The Story of Howsham Mill: restoring an 18ᵗʰ century watermill for 21ˢᵗ century use

Martin Phillips
History chapter by Elaine Gathercole

www.newgeneration-publishing.com

New Generation Publishing

Contents

Foreword

When I was first approached by Dave Mann and Mo MacLeod to become involved with the Renewable Heritage Trust, I was straight away excited by their enthusiasm and determination. As a local landowner with an historical family link to the Howsham Estate, this was a project of great interest to me. It was going to generate a considerable amount of renewable energy, set up an environmental education centre and restore a remarkable historic building. It was a relief to find a charity that had a high chance of earning its own keep.

In the early stages there was always that scrabble for money familiar to anyone who has embarked on such a project, but it soon gathered steam. I joined the bus going to Sussex to shout ourselves hoarse in support of the project in the final of the BBC Restoration programme, in a bid to goad viewers into voting for us. This reflected that huge enthusiasm which gave the scheme such a boost. Large numbers of people, including many tens of trainee soldiers came from far and wide to help dig away the accumulated silt and clear the site.

As Martin describes so well in the book, there were very considerable difficulties on the way. The discouragement felt when thieves repeatedly break in or when promised funds fail to appear can be devastating. It is tempting to say that Dave and Mo soldiered on through thick and thin; they did. But this was a team effort. The Trustees came from all walks of life to contribute what they could. Several have stayed right through from the beginning. Martin himself is one of those who has devoted, and still devotes, so much of his time to managing and running the charity. The mill is open regularly for casual visitors to learn about the project, while primary school groups make good use of the site for learning about the environment.

Not only is this the story of the people and the huge amount of effort that made it happen, it is also a testament to how much people want to contribute to changing the way we produce our electricity. The mill now generates up to 1300 kWh per day, enough to power a small village. Let us hope that the example of the Howsham Mill inspires others to use our rivers in similar fashion. Now that the mill is so beautifully restored, providing power for the grid and an education centre for all ages it is tempting to forget how much was involved in seeing it through to completion; a wonderful example of what can be achieved with enough enthusiasm, cooperation and determination. Let us praise all who contributed to its success.

Sir Fredric Strickland-Constable Bt.
Patron, the Renewable Heritage Trust

Introduction

If Dave Mann had not struggled through the undergrowth blocking the footpath leading to Howsham Mill in November 2003, the likelihood is that by now it would be a pile of stones and bricks. He was over in the UK from Norway, where he had been living with his family, looking for a house to rent in the York area. He was making the move after having been made redundant from his job as a seismic engineer. He had noticed the disused mill on the Ordnance Survey map and, on a whim, had decided to try and find it; he had always liked watermills. The public footpath to the mill is a dead end and few people walked it then. What he found, surrounded by trees and shrubs, were the complete four walls of the main part of the mill, and the remains of the walls of the attached part now called the granary. Neither had a roof and both were filled with rubble, bits of old iron machinery and lots of soil. Another decade or two and one or more of the large crack willow trees nearby, notorious for cracking and blowing over, hence the name, would have fallen in and brought down the walls.

The Interior of the mill when re-discovered looking towards the wheel shaft 2003.
Photo: T Bartholomew.

Dave phoned his wife Mo MacLeod and told her about his find and that he thought they might have a project to start when they moved back. In what Mo later called a 'singular act of lunacy', they decided to buy it. They tracked down the owner, a Mr Burrows, who agreed to sell for £30,000. The building came with the small island on which it stands, an area of about 7000 m². The island is formed by the River Derwent to the west and the now partially silted-up canal to the east. When the river was navigable, barges and boats would pass through the lock, now missing a pair of gates, and along the canal to get around the weir, on their way upstream to Malton and downstream to the River Ouse and beyond.

Dave and Mo's original idea was to restore the mill and turn it into a family home. This was an ambitious plan that was going to take a lot of time and money. The mill is Grade II listed, located in a flood plain and conservation area, and only had a right of access on foot. The building itself is actually quite small with the space required for the waterwheel separating the two parts. It soon became apparent that converting it for residential use would not be practical.

This setback was not going to put them off their project. The logical next step was to form a charity to take on the restoration and to give the building a different use. This would bring together like-minded people with the skills and enthusiasm to start the daunting process of raising the many thousands of pounds that would be needed to get the building habitable, at the very least. Thus the Renewable Heritage Trust (RHT) was formed and registered on 5 July 2004. The objectives of RHT are '...to preserve for the benefit of the people of the locality...buildings of particular beauty or historical, architectural or constructional interest which may, without detriment to the building's heritage, be adapted to generate renewable energy.' For the foreseeable future the one and only project supported by the trust was to be the restoration of Howsham Mill.

The first group of trustees included Dave Mann as treasurer, Mo MacLeod as chair, their neighbour Jane Wegelius, and Jeanie Swales, an old friend from Scarborough. More trustees joined soon after including Pete Anderson, Phil Kershaw, Eileen Barker, Martin Phillips, Paul Lister and Val Hood. A patron was found in Sir Frederic Strickland-Constable. The Strickland family once owned Howsham Hall and the mill. Sir Fred still farms land around Howsham including nearby Paradise Farm. With the formation of the charity, public money could be raised. A membership scheme was started and the initial group of people who parted with £100 each to become life members provided some much-needed start-up capital. Crucially, the formation of RHT meant that the trust could apply for local and national funding to begin work.

Mo and Dave agreed to make over the mill and island to RHT, with an agreement that they would be repaid out of income from electricity sales at some point in the future. In doing this they were putting their faith in the future hydro-electricity potential of the site and in RHT to repay them.

One organisation that provided financial help and support to the fledgling project was the Architectural Heritage Fund. Early on it awarded RHT a £4000 grant towards a feasibility study for restoring the building and consideration of its potential new uses. Staff from the Howardian Hills

Area of Outstanding Natural Beauty (AONB) were also early supporters of the project. The mill is located in the south-east corner of the AONB and restoring an historic building with renewable energy generation potential, run by local people for local benefit, met their criteria for funding.

On the ground the first task was to fell and clear all the trees that were in close proximity to the building and threatened it. The AONB provided half the cost of a group of tree surgeons, who spent three days cutting down the willow, ash and sycamore trees that had started growing once the mill was abandoned. Regular flooding over the previous nearly 60 years had deposited soil and nutrients in which they thrived. Following on was the first volunteer day held on Sunday 27 November 2004. Thus began the long slow process of clearing the vegetation, stacking the logs, shifting fallen masonry and iron work, and what was to become the biggest task, digging soil out of the building, the mill race, the area in front of the wheel and the mill pond. The Howsham Mill restoration project had begun.

First sight of the mill surrounded by trees and shrubs in 2003.
Photo: D Mann.

The history of Howsham Mill

The early history

The restored building seen today was commissioned by the new heir to the Howsham Estate in 1755, Nathaniel Cholmley. The architect was probably John Carr of York, who was then in the early years of what was to become a distinguished career. However, there has been a mill on the site for much longer. The Domesday Book was an inventory of the lands of England that was compiled twenty-two years after the Norman conquest of 1066 and it records there being a mill at Howsham. The site has therefore been used for perhaps a thousand years or more.

Prior to the Norman invasion, the Manor of Howsham was owned by a man called Waltheof. He was ousted and by 1086 it was owned by Robert, Count of Mortain, who was the half-brother of William the Conqueror. By about 1121, the Manor of Howsham was in the hands of a wealthy landowner called Walter l'Espec, who also had extensive lands around Helmsley. At about this time he founded the Priory at Kirkham, a few miles upstream. There is a legend that he did this because his son and heir died in a riding accident. He also gave the monks land and sources of income including the tithes of the Manor of Howsham and specifically the mill, but not ownership. This stayed in the hands of his descendants via Robert de Roos, his sister's son. It remained in the de Roos family until 1508 when is passed to Sir George Manners, who was subsequently made 1st Earl of Rutland.

In 1572, the 3rd Earl of Rutland, Edward Manners, sold the Manor of Howsham to Thomas Bamburgh for £2100. The latter seems to have been an important servant of the Earls of Rutland. The family thrived and in 1610 Sir William Bamburgh built Howsham Hall, probably on the site of an earlier manor house and supposedly using stone from Kirkham Priory, following its dissolution by Henry VIII.

Sir William died in 1623 and as his two sons had died before him, the lands around Howsham were split between a daughter and two of his grandsons. One of these, Thomas Wentworth, inherited the Hall and watermill. The mill stayed in the Wentworth family until the death of Sir Butler Cavendish Wentworth in 1741, who died childless.

A map dated 1705 shows that the land around Howsham had been enclosed. On it are marked the mill, the weir and the village, which consisted of two rows of cottages; today there is only one row on the east side of the road.

Howsham Hall then passed to Sir Butler's half-sister, Catherine Wentworth, who had married Hugh Cholmley of Whitby. In 1755 their son Nathaniel Cholmley inherited both the Whitby and Howsham Estates and decided to move his family to Howsham and make it their main country residence.

The mill is about 500 m from the Hall and at the time there would have been a clear sight line between the two. Perhaps the old mill was a bit of an eye-sore and a striking new building would make a statement about the Hall's new occupant. It is in the Gothic style with ogee arches above the doors and windows, detailed crocketed finials at each corner of the pyramid roof and dormer windows in the same style. The lead statue of Diana, the Roman and Greek goddess of hunting, mounted on the apex of the roof, suggests that it was designed to look like a hunting lodge in the grounds of the Hall. The precise date of construction is not known but was between 1755 and 1757. The latter date is inscribed by the left-hand edge of the window to the right of the south door. A stone set in the sluice of the weir is inscribed 'Repaired by IB Dilliner 1759', suggesting work was taking place at that time. Evidence in a legal case in 1791 said that the ancient mill was demolished and a new one built about the time the witness left Howsham in 1757. A sketch of the mill made in 1807 shows it to be much as it is today.

Howsham Mill soon after it was abandoned in 1947. Note the detail that has been reproduced in the restoration. The original lead figure of Diana is at the apex of the roof.

Albert Fox returned to the mill after more than 60 years. He is talking to Mo MacLeod and Geraldine Mathieson in front of the hearth before restoration work began.
Photo: M Phillips.

In the mid-1770s improvements were made to the Hall. The famous landscape architect Capability Brown was commissioned to re-design the landscape around the Hall. The mill forms one point of a potential geometric design, a line linking a now missing tower to the north-east in the nearby woods through the Hall to the mill. A second line was from Crambe Grange on the other side of the river, through the Hall to the Orangery. This was a technique often used by Brown. Thus the mill would have been a major feature of the new parkland. During this period the row of dwellings on the east side of the village was demolished. This was probably because they interfered with the aesthetics of the newly designed landscape.

Nathaniel Cholmley died in 1791 and was succeeded first by his brother and then soon after, by his daughter Catherine, whose husband took the Cholmley name. By 1874 the Hall was in the hands of Sir Charles Strickland, one of Cholmley's great grandsons by his second wife. On his death aged 90 in 1909, it passed to his daughter, Esther Anne Willoughby.

A newspaper article from 1926 mentions the mill as hidden by trees. Perhaps by now it was not the feature it had once been. The article described the figure of an archer (Diana) on the roof and also a 'sinister' sundial above the south door, just visible in a photograph from the 1960s but now lost. "*The pointing finger stands out to form the nose of the evil face that is painted round it; a red face with yellowy-blue eyes, the whole smeared with black."*

In 1940, Mrs Willoughby died without an heir and Howsham Hall passed to her sister-in-law and husband's niece, the Hon Mrs Ida Mary Hazel Strickland, née Willoughby who was married to Captain H Strickland. In 1947 the mill ceased operations and in 1948 the Hall was sold and stood empty. In the early 1950s the latter was threatened with demolition. However, the building was rescued in 1956 when it was bought by Mr Knock who turned it into a preparatory school that opened two years later. The school closed in 2007 when it was sold to a developer and restored back to a private house. It is currently leased by a company that hires it out for weddings and other functions.

In 1965 the mill and the island were sold to Bradford No. 1 Angling Association. In the same year the mill too was threatened with demolition due to its unsafe condition, the result of a fire that had destroyed the roof. Fortunately, in 1966 it was Grade II listed, which prevented it from being lost altogether. Over the years some of the metal work was removed for its scrap value, including most of the lead statue of Diana. In 1991 the mill and island were bought by Mr Burrows. It was to be another twelve years before the next phase in the life of the mill began.

The operations of the mill

Howsham Mill, like hundreds of watermills and windmills across the country, closed because it had become redundant. From 1905, it had only processed grain for animal feed; large mills were by then producing flour for bread-making. After the Second World War, farms in the area were connected to the electricity grid and were able to process their own grain for livestock feed with simple electric-powered mill and mix systems. From the remaining machinery and stones, and using diagrams of other similar watermills, the operation at Howsham can be deduced.

Water from above the weir fed through a gate that could control flow into the mill chamber. The wheel, steel from the mid-19th century, wooden before that, sat in a brick-lined chamber mounted on bearings. The wheel's axle extended east into the main mill through a tall opening. A roughly triangular platform made of brick covered with stone flags projected from the west wall at ground level. This is now gone but indicated by the new layout of flagstones. In the centre of the platform is a rectangular pit which currently accommodates one of the bearings supporting the axle. Behind the platform is a second deeper pit which would have once accommodated the bevelled pit wheel. It was in two sections bolted around a hexagonal drive fixed on the axle. The pit wheel would have in turn operated the wallower wheel, set at right angles and creating a vertical drive. The upright shaft was wooden for the bottom 4 ft then iron to the top. The vertical drive would have turned a great bevelled spur wheel above the pit wheel and this would have in turn, operated the stone nuts at the base of the mill stones, thus turning them to grind the corn. The great spur wheel was of iron, not wood. Above the mill stones, it is likely that there was a crown wheel which turned an auxiliary north-south horizontal drive shaft (the transmission box for which remains in the north wall) and which could be used to operate other machines and mechanisms in the mill, such as the sack hoist. The crown wheel was made of wood with iron spokes.

Towards the north end of the west wall of the main building, near ground floor level, there is an opening with an arched header, now fitted with a window. This opened onto the wheelhouse and probably held a winding crane for adjusting the sluice gate in front of the wheelhouse.

There were at least two pairs of stones in operation and possibly a third. The stones came from three different sources and include lava stone, Derbyshire millstone grit and French burr stone made of quartzite quarried in the Paris basin. Rather than being made in one piece, the latter consist of segments set in plaster of Paris and bound with iron bands. Howsham also had what appeared to be a cake-crusher and another machine whose purpose was uncertain.

The main building had two storeys and a loft. The north-east corner of the main room was chamfered forming a chimney for an open fire. It now houses a small stove. At ground floor level on the south side there are three small holes which run through to the exterior and drain water from the building after a flood. Modified, they still serve this purpose.

In 1794 there was a very large payment of around £224 for repairs, compared to the much smaller repair costs of between £2 and £17 in the following years. The miller's annual salary was only £20 in the period 1792 - 1800 and the cost of the repair was also more than the mill made. Between 1793 and 1808 income was between £120 and £180 a year, though this rose to between £230 and £270 in 1809 - 1811. There is no information regarding what the high repair bill was for, but it is possible that it was for an early replacement wheel. The autumn of 1794 was the wettest for 20 years, so flooding may have been a factor.

In a newspaper article from 1947 the author describes entering the mill:

"As the heavy oak door swung inwards, I noticed the sun dial above. Rats scurried away as we went within. A little barley meal had been left in the vat above. The ladders and floors were shaky. Old grinding stones, worn thin with use, lay propped against the walls, but the huge circular stones in use up to a few weeks ago, were in excellent condition. So was the wheel."

Albert Fox, who returned to the mill in September 2011, recalled as a boy bringing grain by horse and cart from Mount Pleasant Farm in Welburn to be ground at the mill. He remembered queuing up to cross the swing bridge. The cart went round to the granary to unload its sacks of corn. The driver then had to back the horse and cart as there was insufficient room to turn on the west side. There was a large iron ring outside the building to which the horse was tied while their driver waited for the corn to be ground. In its last years the huge iron door key was kept in a fork of an old ash tree that still stands close to the building.

The millers

We have a fairly good idea of who the millers were for most of the period from 1721 until the closure of the mill. Some of them were tenants who paid a rent to the owner of £60 to £70 a year in the 18th century, while others were paid a salary of £20 to £25 a year in the early 19th century. Some were from local families, either from Howsham or nearby villages, whereas others were from further afield, sometimes with previous experience of milling and sometimes going on to work at other mills. In some cases the miller worked the mill for 20 to 30 years and either took over from or handed it on to, another family member. In other cases, a miller was only there for a few years. There is no evidence for any of them living at the mill. The last miller was Johnny Braithwaite. He took on the job in September 1946 but continued only until the following summer. That winter had been a terrible one, with long periods of sub-zero temperatures and deep snow. This must have prevented farmers reaching the mill and working conditions would have been bad. Perhaps the experience encouraged him to make the decision to emigrate to Australia. Prior to that, Carl Carr was the miller from 1919 up to his retirement in 1946. An invoice from his tenure dated 1944, shows that he rolled a total of 1029 stones (655 kg) of barley, oats and beans for Mr Featherstone of nearby Crambe Grange over a six-month period and charged him £3/16/11 (£3.81). In that year, barley was worth £27 per ton and oats £15 per ton.

It seems that in some periods the millers could augment their income by being paid two guineas a year by the Fitzwilliams of Malton, to open the lock and the wooden swing bridge on the cut to allow boats through.

Newspaper articles from 1863 and 1872 stated that millers had been allowed to take fish from the river, even earning up to £12 a year from the sale of eels. Any salmon had to be sent to the Hall, though none had been caught recently. A fifteen-pounder caught in 1847 earned the miller £1/2/6. The fish and eels were trapped in hecks – boxes set in the sluice where the first screw now sits. A watercolour of the mill from 1807 shows these located in the weir.

Creating the island

An Act of Parliament of 1702 provided for making the River Derwent navigable from its mouth up to Yedingham, above Malton. As part of this process, in 1720 an unlikely combination of Joshua Mitchell, an innkeeper from Castleford, and Mark Andrews, a carpenter from Wakefield, signed a contract to do the necessary work to make the river navigable to Malton for the sum of £4000. The agreement gave a detailed specification for what was to be done at Howsham. This included digging the cut, building a lock exactly the same as the one to be built at Kirkham and making "*a good and sufficient wood bridge over the said lock for horses to pass over the same to the mills at Howsham*". On 20th May 1721 there is a note that they "*began to dig at Kirkham*" and nine days later they paid for 1329 yards of ground (probably cubic yards) to be cut at Howsham – paying 2d a yard, a total cost of just over £11.

The developers also had to create a hauling way or tow path alongside the river. The boats which initially used the navigation were pulled by men, not horses. Later, in 1756, the tow path was improved so horses could be used. It was on the east side of the river to the mill, then crossed to the west side up to Kirkham. This meant that the horses had to go back to the road bridge to get to the other side of the river. This change was probably so that the tow path did not pass by the rear of the Hall.

Initially the locks were designed to take craft up to 55 ft long and 14 ft wide. Improvements allowed slightly larger Yorkshire keels and sloops to pass through. The main cargo was coal from the West Riding of Yorkshire to Malton, and corn from the arable fields of the East Riding on the return journey.

The navigation was owned by the Fitzwilliam family. By the end of the 18th and start of the 19th century trade on the river was brisk. There were 35 vessels operating up to Malton, two sloops plying trade between Malton and Hull and a further 14 vessels that did not go as far as Malton. A round trip from Malton to Leeds took about three weeks. This meant that around 20 vessels a week passed through the Howsham lock and swing bridge. Tolls collected amounted to about £6500 per year. However, this all began to change with the opening of the York to Scarborough railway in 1845. It was built by George Hudson, the railway king who coincidentally was born in Howsham village, and George and Robert Stephenson. They had under-estimated costs and over-estimated income so struggled initially to make a profit. The railway company managed to gain control of the navigation, tolls were raised on the latter and traffic declined such that by 1890 the only regular trade was on the lower reaches of the river.

By the early 1900s the river was used mainly by pleasure craft. Floods in 1930 badly damaged the gates of the lock at Kirkham and it was closed permanently by 1932. Then in 1935 the navigation rights on the River Derwent were revoked by parliament. The reason cited was the conflict between land drainage and the need to keep water levels high for navigation. If field drain and ditch outfalls were frequently below the river level, the land would remain wet.

In the early 1970s, The Yorkshire Derwent Trust was formed to try and re-open the river to navigation. It gained leases on several locks, including the one at Howsham and in 1974 repairs were made to it and the weir. Photographs from that date show volunteers clearing and repairing the lock and opening up the cut; in one the original swing bridge can just be seen. As explained in the next chapter, navigation rights were not re-instated and today the only boats on the river are canoes and kayaks with the permission of the adjoining landowners.

The River Derwent

Navigation

The River Derwent rises on the eastern side of the North York Moors and flows towards Scarborough but is prevented from reaching the sea by glacial deposits, so turns west running through the Vale of Pickering. The River Rye drains land on the western side of the North York Moors and joins the Derwent above Malton and about doubles the volume of water then flowing down the river. The Vale of Pickering was once a lake formed when the ice melted at the end of the last ice age about 13,000 years ago. The water forced its way out through the small gorge at Kirkham, flowing on past Howsham and Stamford Bridge, through Elvington east of York and into the lower Derwent valley. Here, adjacent to the river, are old traditional ings or flood meadows. The Derwent joins the River Ouse below Selby at Barmby.

There is some evidence that the river was navigated perhaps as far back as Roman times. Where the first Archimedes Screw is sited was once a flash lock. This was simple way of backing water up above the weir behind a gate, opening the gate to release the flow of water on which the craft was pulled up by men with ropes. This was slow and laborious and limited river traffic. The solution was to dig a canal and construct a lock around each weir. Following the establishment of the Derwent Navigation Act by parliament in 1702, the necessary locks and canals were built and trade up and down the river increased. However, when the York to Scarborough railway line was opened in 1845, river traffic declined and largely ended after 1935 when the navigation rights were revoked.

A decision made in 1970 in the House of Commons that, if it had gone the other way, would have made a big change to the river. There was a bill before parliament to approve construction of a reservoir on the North York Moors. It would have flooded half of Farndale by damming the tributary that eventually flows into the Derwent. This was considered necessary to control the supply of water downstream to allow more abstraction for domestic and industrial uses in urban parts of Yorkshire. The bill passed its second reading. In the committee stage, the chairman used his casting vote against the bill and the scheme was not passed into law, thus preventing what would have been a major change to both Farndale and the character of the river.

In the late 1970s a long dispute began over navigation along the Derwent. Boating interests supported by Malton Town Council wanted to re-open navigation above Sutton. Below here the river is tidal and thus there is a right of navigation. The plan was to build a marina at Malton and various leisure facilities along the river. A barrage at the mouth of the river at Barmby was opened in 1972 to control the flow of water in and out, thus enabling extraction at Elvington and Loftsome Bridge. New embankments along the lower reaches of the river to control flooding and provide deeper water facilitated navigation. The plan was opposed by conservation interests led by the Yorkshire Wildlife Trust, anglers and a group of riparian landowners. The arguments were protracted and complicated, based on the detail of previous parliamentary Acts, historical records and old maps. The case was heard in the High Court in London in 1988. Finally, over a year later, the defendants, i.e. the conservationists, heard that they had won the case, but the plaintiffs immediately appealed. Both sides again made their arguments in the Appeal Court in London. The appeal was upheld on one point, that rivers and lakes were public rights of way. If this judgement stood, many lowland rivers and waterways would become open to boat traffic. Despite the mounting legal costs, the defendants sought leave to appeal and the case went to the House of Lords, then the highest court in the land. The five law lords unanimously agreed with the conservationists over the definition of a river and in 1991 the case was finally settled. For a detailed description of these events and much more about the river see *The Yorkshire River Derwent* by Ian Carstairs.

The wildlife of the river and island

The River Derwent from Rye mouth above Malton to its confluence with the River Ouse, was designated a Site of Special Scientific Interest (SSSI) in 1986, along with some adjacent land, in particular flood meadows in the lower Derwent valley, for the plants and animals they support. The mill island was also included in the SSSI. Two European designations, Special Area of Conservation (SAC) for habitats and Special Protection Area (SPA) for the bird life have also been applied, the latter to the lower Derwent valley. The Derwent is considered one of the best lowland rivers in England for its wildlife and scenic beauty. Excess siltation and high phosphate levels, primarily due to soil run-off from agricultural land, mean much of the river is currently considered in what is described as 'unfavourable recovering condition'. Efforts are being made to reduce the amount of soil entering the river and to address other issues through the Yorkshire River Derwent Catchment Partnership.

One of the reasons the river was designated a SSSI is because of its aquatic vegetation. Among the more important plants for supporting invertebrates, the organisms at the base of the food-chain, is water crowfoot. It is a member of the buttercup family and its characteristic leaves and flowers appear on the surface of the river in summer. There are particularly good beds both immediately above and below Howsham weir.

Water crowfoot in the river above the weir with the mill and wheel race behind.
Photo: M Phillips

In order to get a licence to install the Archimedes Screw turbine, the first in the UK, the Environment Agency (EA) required evidence of what happened to fish that passed through the screw. Data from Germany indicated that fish were unharmed by the experience. RHT commissioned consultants to carry out such a study. They first caught fish by a process called electro-fishing. A rod emitting a small electric charge is held in the water and fish are attracted to it. They are stunned by the charge, allowing them to be netted out of the river and held in an aerated storage tank. The fish soon come round, unaffected by their experience. Within a couple of hours,

A male kingfisher on his perch.

nearly 200 individuals of fourteen different species had been collected. Pike, chub, grayling and roach were the commonest species. Also included were brown trout, one salmon, bullhead, one eel and several river lamprey. Individuals were inspected and measured before being dropped in the water flowing into the screw. The screw threads around a cylinder that sits in a trough and water flows in columns either side of the cylinder. Once passed the leading edge of the thread, there is no risk of a fish being injured. After passing through the screw, the fish were caught in a net set at the base. Once again they were inspected before being released. None showed any signs of injury as a result of their ordeal.

To help migratory species such as trout and salmon move up the river, the EA is proposing to construct a fish pass on the weir adjacent to the two screws. The fish on their journey upstream are attracted to the water rushing out of the screws. Indeed at just that position, a large salmon was seen leaping up the weir in October 2016. It made a few attempts but was not successful. The ladder would have allowed it to progress part way up the weir, rest and then try again.

One species of particular interest is the river lamprey. This is a primitive eel-like fish with a sucker mouth. The young lamprey, called transformers, feed for several years in the mud at the bottom of the river before migrating out to sea where they have a parasitic phase. The lamprey attaches itself to a trout or salmon using hooks around its mouth, sucking blood from the host, but not killing it. It returns attached to the fish to spawn in gravel beds in the river in spring. Research funded by Mannpower Hydro in 2009 and carried out by scientists from Durham University, involved catching transformers moving downstream in nets to estimate the proportion that might flow through the screw. They also put a sample of transformers and one adult through the screw and recovered as many as possible in a net. None of the lamprey was killed or injured during its passage. RHT has worked with Natural England to inform canoeists about the importance of the water crowfoot beds and the spawning sites of lamprey so that damage to these habitats is avoided.

Another important and charismatic species found on the river, and on rivers throughout the UK, is the otter. The aquatic mammal has made a remarkable recovery in England in recent decades. They were reintroduced onto the River Derwent in the mid-1980s, partly because it was an undisturbed and unpolluted river. Yet on the same river otters were hunted up until the 1950s. Seeing one is partly down to luck, but patience and regular observation also help. There have been quite a few sightings on the stretch of river by the weir. Several times they have been seen feeding on the weir where they are looking for snails and other invertebrates. Their favourite food is the eel, but they will eat all sorts of fish and even birds.

Including the island in the SSSI was a bit of an anomaly in what is an aquatic habitat – the river. But the boundary line was drawn down the canal, not the bank of the river and that means what RHT does on the island has to be agreed with Natural England. The vegetation on the island does not have any special ecological interest. It is mixed deciduous woodland with ash, crack willow and sycamore the dominant tree species. There is also alder, oak, wych elm, hawthorn, elder and field maple. Soon after RHT acquired the island, a plant survey was carried out and 94 species of herbaceous plant were identified. There are species that are indicative of old woodland such as dog's mercury, lords and ladies, wood anemone and wild garlic or ramsones.

A number of damp-loving species are found along the banks of the river and canal including reed sweet-grass, flag iris, yellow-cress, water figwort, meadowsweet and gipsywort. Aggressive species such a stinging nettle have thrived, probably due to the regular flooding over the years and the deposition of silt from the river. The silt adds nutrients, particularly phosphate that favours the fast-growing species. The invasive alien Himalayan balsam is common on the banks all along river. It is an aggressive annual plant that dominates the flora during the summer, then dies back in winter leaving bare soil that is at risk of erosion. The seeds float along the water and germinate where they land on soil. Each year volunteers attempt to pull balsam, but there is too much of it to make much effect. Another alien plant found along the banks of the river is giant hogweed. When it is seen on the island, it is immediately dug up and destroyed. The ground around the building is kept mown to allow visitors access. Another section of the island within the woodland is for forest school activities and here there is very little ground vegetation due to all the trampling by little feet.

Having taken advice and using our own experience, the management policy is to maintain the woodland cover, but with some thinning of sycamore to allow the native ash to become the dominant tree species and to let in more light for the benefit of the ground flora. In the early years a few oak saplings were planted and ash regeneration is left, though this has suffered from ash die-back disease.

An important component of woodland is dead wood, both as standing trees and fallen logs. These are left where possible and safe to do so. Lots of different fungi and a whole range of invertebrates live in the decaying wood. Bug hunting under logs has become a popular activity by visiting school groups. Experts have helped identify some of the many species of slugs and snails found on the island.

Observations and trapping in mist nets by licensed experts has produced a list of 65 bird species seen on or near the island. Woodland birds include five species of tit, nuthatch, tree creeper, robin, wren, dunnock and chaffinch. Willow warbler, garden warbler, sedge warbler, reed warbler, Cetti's warbler, chiffchaff, blackcap, whitethroat and spotted flycatcher are welcome summer visitors. Mute swan, mallard and moorhen occur regularly on the river and grey wagtail nest nearby each summer. Sometimes a cormorant or grey heron will be seen and occasionally the blue flash of a kingfisher flying by. A bird hide built by volunteers at the top of the island was a good place to watch activity on the river, the weir and the canal; sadly, it was burnt down by vandals in 2020. A number of bird boxes was put up and are used regularly. Bat boxes have been occupied by mice, but so far not by bats. However, there is usually a summer breeding roost of soprano pipistrelles in the roof of the granary. Daubenton's bats, which skim along the surface of the river feeding on insects, and noctule bats have been recorded by observers using detectors that pick up the ultrasound signals they make when hunting their insect prey.

Realising the hydro-power potential

For centuries, the force exerted by flowing water has been used to power equipment such as turning stones to grind wheat and other grains into a form that humans and animals can consume. Where there was a significant fall of water, such as a stream or river flowing down an incline, or over a weir built in a river to create a fall, the gravitational energy of the falling water has been turned into mechanical force to drive the equipment. Quite when the weir at Howsham was first constructed is not recorded. But for as long as there has been a mill, there must have been a weir.

The bend in the river and its widening must have been considered a good location to build a weir. The purpose of a weir on a lowland river such as the Derwent is to increase the fall and thus the gravitational energy in the water flowing over. Although gravity is taking the river down to the sea, the force is not very large. The river, where it enters the lowlands of the Vale of Pickering at West Ayton, is at about 35 m above sea level; at Howsham it is 12 m, a distance of about 45 km (28 miles) and a drop of only 51 cm per km. To turn a wheel or other form of turbine, the force needs to be increased and this is done by creating an artificial drop called the head. In the case of Howsham weir the head is 1.75 m at its maximum, though will vary considerably based on the level of the water above and more importantly, below the weir. The average flow of water over the total width of the weir is something like 35 cubic metres per second (cumec), varying due to rainfall over the river catchment. A cubic metre of water weighs 1000 kg or 1 tonne, so up to 35 t of water is passing over the weir every second. Only a small proportion of this can be diverted through a waterwheel or Archimedes Screw turbine, and it is this flow of water multiplied by the head that gives the output in kilowatts (kW) of electricity.

Assessing the potential

The potential for a small-scale hydro-electricity scheme at Howsham clearly existed as had been demonstrated by the waterwheel turning for hundreds of years. The wheel would only have used a fraction of the energy flowing by in the river as it would have operated for just a few hours a day at most. A generator connected to a refurbished wheel could operate twenty-four hours a day, seven days a week, given a suitable river level. The existing sluice also had the potential to take another turbine. This potential was recognised by Dave Mann, who was looking for a change in direction in his career away from the oil industry to renewable forms of power. Small-scale hydro was relatively undeveloped in the UK compared to solar photo-voltaic and wind turbines. There was interest from the government and the Renewable Obligation Certificate (ROC) system was introduced in 2002 to provide a financial incentive to all types of renewable electricity generation. This was replaced by the Feed-in Tariff (FiT) in 2010. The scheme has now ended for new systems but will be paid on existing ones for 20 years. The FiT is paid on every kWh of electricity generated and, in addition, the wholesale electricity price is paid on what is exported. Small turbines have been in use for many years such as the Francis turbine, but these will injure or kill fish that pass through them. To avoid harm, fish must be prevented from entering the turbine, which necessitates a screen with a mesh small enough to exclude them. At Howsham this would have required a bar spacing of no more than 2.5 mm. The fine screen would need to be very large and would have the disadvantage of collecting debris and so blocking the flow of water, requiring an efficient system to keep it clear.

Dave decided to research alternatives to these existing turbines and came across the use of the Archimedes Screw in Germany. This is a screw with a very wide spiral thread around a cylinder sitting in a trough, with only a very small gap between the thread and the trough. The principle of the Archimedes Screw is more than 2000 years old. It was invented as a means of lifting water from a river or other source to a higher level. Often this was for irrigating fields adjacent to a river. Today they are still used this way for lifting water. To do this, a mechanical force has to be applied to turn the screw. In the past that force may have been a donkey or camel. Today it would be an electric motor. Reversing the flow so that the water turns the screw allowing it to turn a generator, is a recent innovation. As the screw turns slowly at about 30 rpm, a gearbox also needs to be installed between the screw and the generator to increase the output speed to generate electricity. The Archimedes Screw turbine had been shown to be efficient at sites with a low head of between 1 m and 10 m.

With the basis for a hydro scheme, the next step was to discuss these ideas with the Environment Agency (EA), the government body charged with looking after rivers in England. This was to be the start of a long, slow process to convince the relevant staff in the EA that the plans were achievable, would not harm wildlife in and around the river, would not affect the fishing rights owned by local fishing clubs or public enjoyment of this stretch of the river. Also consulted early on was the project officer for the River Derwent SSSI at English Nature, which would later become Natural England. Crucially, studies in Germany had shown that the Archimedes Screw turbine did not harm fish that passed through it. Our own study, demanded by the EA, was carried out in April 2009 by fisheries consultants. The details of this are described in the chapter about the River Derwent. The study would confirm, unsurprisingly, that British fish, like German fish, also passed through unharmed. This avoided the need for a fine screen to exclude them. To prevent larger debris and animals (and humans) from entering, all that would be needed was a series of vertical bars with a spacing of 13 cm. This still has to be kept clear by raking and physically removing branches, leaves and whatever else is floating down the river.

Realising the potential

At the same time as convincing the authorities, there had to be a sound business case to support the proposal. This would be the first project that Dave Mann's fledgling business, Mannpower Hydro, would develop and there was a lot to be learnt along the way. The resulting proposal was for a restored waterwheel, using the existing shaft mounted on two new bearings, with new spokes and new paddles. In the process of excavating the wheel race, several of the original paddles were recovered and used as templates to construct new ones. There was room for two Archimedes Screw turbines to go in the existing sluice, after repairs and modifications. These would be rated at 25 kW each and the waterwheel at 15 kW. A budget prepared in 2006 suggested a return on capital of between 3.9% and 7.9% depending on how many turbines were installed.

Raising the capital was going to be a challenge. The first system to work on was the wheel. This was an integral part of the building – you couldn't have a watermill without a waterwheel. Staff at the Howardian Hills AONB were very supportive of the restoration of the building and had a strong interest in renewable electricity generation. These two interests came together in funding the restoration of the wheel. Pete McKew, who ran a small agricultural engineering company called Dockend in Whitby and had restored his own waterwheel, took on the job of doing the same for the one at Howsham. This involved making new spokes and paddles to bolt onto the existing cast iron shaft. The shaft itself was mounted on original refurbished brass bush bearings. Prior to this the wheel race had been completely cleared of the remains of the old wheel and a copious quantity of silt and debris. This allowed the walls to be repaired and repointed, using reclaimed bricks and waterproof hydraulic lime mortar. The work was done by stonemason Geoff Hutchinson, who would later work on restoring the granary.

Getting the new parts of the wheel to site would be one of the first uses for the newly purchased pontoon. Access to the site was seen as a problem early on. The solution seemed to be to use the river, but what sort of craft could do the job? The answer was a pontoon made up of sections of tough plastic each 0.25 cubic metre that could be joined together to make any desired size and shape. To avoid any pollution, one or two electric outboard motors powered by 12 v batteries could be fitted to propel it along the river. The wheel sections were delivered to the Stephenson's farm upstream from the mill. Tom Stephenson kindly loaded them onto the pontoon and on Sunday 7 May 2006 it set off downstream with a crew of three. After a short and uneventful journey, the pontoon moored just above the weir. There was still a large blockage of soil in front of the wheel chamber and this kept the site dry while the wheel was put together. A sluice gate was also needed and this too was installed. It would eventually be hydraulically driven, but for now it could be opened by a ratchet. A hand-installed coffer dam of interlocking plastic panels was knocked into the mud at the bottom of the river, supplemented with sandbags filled with soil from in front of the wheel. This diverted water away from the sluice and the wheel race - but not before water had flowed through the wheel and turned it again after nearly 60 years. This was the first step in once more harnessing the power of the river, this time for electricity generation.

Funding for the new screws proved more of a challenge. Dave learnt about a potential source from the government through the Clear Skies Fund. A grant of £50,000 was offered to RHT, not enough for the planned two screws, just the one. Concurrently an application for an abstraction licence had been submitted to the EA for sufficient water for two screws and the wheel. An abstraction licence is needed even if water is just diverted through a structure and back into the river. As the licence was for a type of turbine never before installed in the UK, the process of consultation with river users and concerned organisations was slow. The grant offer had been extended but would expire by end of February 2007. However, there was a lead time of ordering the screw from German company Ritz-Atro of three months. The trustees decided to take a risk and order the screw without the abstraction licence in place. The latter was finally granted on 26 October 2006, but it then transpired that the planning permission for the screws would have to go through the whole consultation process again, not just be added to the permission already granted to restore the mill.

Fortune favours the bold. Permissions and grant finally came together and on 19 February 2007 the screw arrived on the back of a truck from Germany. Steel decking had been laid on the grass field on the far side of the river, thanks to the permission of our patron. A crane hired to lift the screw off the truck eventually arrived and as darkness fell, the 9.5 t screw was hoisted off the truck and onto the pontoon. Austin Lloyd, whose day job was building rides at Flamingo Land, was the 'Person in Charge of Lifting Operation'. He safely ensured the unloading went without a hitch.

The next day, five men and two dogs (literally) set off upstream on the pontoon. A large rope had been laid from a tree island just below the weir to the bridge. By pulling on this rope, which was then coiled on the pontoon, and with the two electric outboard motors pushing and steering, the pontoon made its way slowly up the river and docked by the end of the sluice, where it was secured. Austin and volunteers had built a structure made from stacks of old railway sleepers (loaned from the North York Moors Railway) and upright steel posts bolted onto the concrete, to support two girders across the width of the sluice and one girder along the length. By lifting and pulling the screw using manual chain hoists, it was eased into place over the next few days. The sluice had been prepared in advance to take the screw by repairing brickwork and casting a concrete block for the top end of the screw to sit on. The far end of the sluice was excavated as deep as possible to give the required angle needed to maximise the fall of water through the screw. In the end the angle was not as steep as ideal but was all that could be achieved with hand tools. A vertical sluice gate of wooden boards held together by steel bands, which could be operated up and down by hydraulic pump, had also been installed.

Once the wheel and screw were in place, they then had to be connected to generators. In most situations, the turbine turning at between 10 and 30 rpm would drive a gearbox that would step up the output speed to at least 1000 rpm to run the generator. The position of the wheel shaft was below floor level in an existing pit in the granary. It was inevitable that at some point in the future the granary would flood and the equipment would be inundated. There would be a high risk of water getting in the generator and damaging it. To avoid this, Dave proposed using a hydraulic pump to turn a hydraulic motor attached to the generator sat above flood level, both of which could be housed in a steel cabinet within the granary. Also in this cabinet would be the control panel for the wheel system and the hydraulic pump to operate the two gates.

A similar hydraulic drive was also proposed for the screw as this would allow the speed of the screw to be varied to optimise the output. A quotation for suitable equipment was obtained from a Swedish company Hagglunds, to be installed by local firm, Janguss Hydraulics. Janguss looked at the Hagglunds proposal and said they could design a hydraulic pump to fit on the end of the wheel shaft and a similar arrangement for the screw. Pipes would be buried and run from the screw to another generator driven by a hydraulic motor in the cabinet. They began with the pump for the screw at a cost of £28,634, 90% of which was paid in instalments during its manufacture and bench testing. The company were due to fit and commission it soon after the screw was installed but kept delaying. It was finally fitted and connected up to the motor, but insufficient pressure could be achieved. The engineers took it away and said they would modify it and try again. They returned and refitted it, a job in itself as it weighed several hundred kilos, connected it up, but still there was insufficient pressure to run the motor on the generator. A few weeks later, RHT was informed that the company had gone into liquidation. There was no prospect of recouping any of the money already paid out and RHT was left with a useless lump of steel and a loss of nearly £26,000.

By now Dave was developing contacts in Europe and was able to locate and buy a second-hand gearbox and generator for about £4000. Without

Trainee soldiers digging the soil from in front of the wheel race.
Photo: T Bartholomew.

The new waterwheel and gate fitted in the wheel race July 2006.

Photo: T Bartholomew.

these the screw would be useless so we decided to take a risk and hope that the generator would stay above any flood level. This has not been the case and three times it has been partially submerged, but on each all occasion it was successfully dried out and worked again. Finally, by October 2008 the screw was generating electricity and powering the building. It would take another year to sort out the problems with the wheel and get it working as well.

The main repair that has been made to screw 1 is to replace the lower bearing, which spent much of the time below water and cannot be greased. A different type of oil-filled bearing was fitted which allows any ingress of water to be measured and rectified. This was done in December 2014 at cost of £6500.

Screw 1 coming up the river on the pontoon 2007.

Photo: T Bartholomew.

Screw 1 in the sluice showing the supporting structures used to get it in position.
Photo: M Phillips.

Connecting to the grid

The screw was now working well and producing more electricity than required for the building, but it was not yet possible to sell the surplus to the grid. The problem was the cost of a grid connection and difficulty in getting an agreement for the cable to go under the land belonging to Howsham Hall. There is a high voltage cable running along the road that crosses Howsham Bridge, about 400 m from the mill. Laying a cable and making the connection was going to cost a lot. Very fortuitously, RHT learnt of a grant for which our need was a perfect fit - to connect watermills or windmills to the grid, available from Grantscape. An application was submitted and RHT was awarded £62,000, which covered the cost of the new connection at Howsham Bridge along with the main power cable, control equipment and electrical works required.

The armoured cable had to be buried in a trench 90 cm deep. The new owner of Howsham Hall gave permission for it to be laid under his land. As usual, digging the trench was done the hard way, by trainee soldiers using shovels. The cable also had to cross the mill race and go under the canal. The latter required blocking off the water flow into the canal with a coffer dam and putting in a pump to remove any leakage. Digging deep enough into the mud was almost impossible. Eventually a plastic pipe was laid and buried through which the cable could be fed. After many hours of hard digging over successive Sundays, the trench was ready and the cable arrived on a large wooden reel to be rolled out. Also needed was a transformer to connect with the grid. Dave had hoped to use one that would have sat unobtrusively on a concrete platform, but NEDL, the company responsible for the connection, did not approve this type and insisted on a pole-mounted transformer. It could potentially be obtrusive in the protected landscape around the mill, and representatives from both RDC and the AONB objected to it. This delay in agreeing to its location meant that a section of the cable was lying in the trench until a decision was made. Thieves had noticed this and one night in September 2009 the exposed 60 m section of cable was cut off and stolen. The thieves then went down to the mill and saw through the window various copper items. They smashed down the top half of the stable door into the granary and stole the hot water tank and all the copper piping. Trustees who discovered this theft the next morning felt sick to their stomachs. All the voluntary effort put into the project treated with such contempt, just for a bit of scrap copper. Soon after this incident, agreement was reached with the officials as to where the pole should go - nestled between trees and barely visible. Once again, we picked ourselves up and got on with repairing the cable and the damage to the granary, now with the addition of a barred security gate in front of the door.

The goal of the hydro scheme was to be connected to the grid so that surplus electricity, the majority generated, could be exported and sold. Not only would the project be contributing to the increasing amount of renewable electricity being produced in the UK, it would also provide RHT with an income estimated at about £30,000 per year. This income would be used to run the project and provide funds towards the second phase of the restoration, the main part of the mill. On 26 February 2010 this goal was achieved.

With the screw generating, we turned our attention again to the waterwheel system. A local engineering company called BDC Ltd showed interest and said that they could utilise some of the parts from the existing hydraulic system. They proposed to modify the end of the original cast iron shaft, fit a tollock (a type of coupling) to connect it via a large gearbox and hydraulic pump to the hydraulic pump and generator we had available. This combination was fitted and running by the summer of 2010, but it was rather noisy and less efficient than expected. All seemed to be going well until the end of the year when the system had to be shut down due to a worrying noise – the new pump had failed. Rather than replace it, the decision was made to drop the whole idea of hydraulic drive for the generator. A new 15 kW immersion proof (IP67 rated) generator was available that could be connected via the gearbox to the wheel shaft. This was fitted by BDC and running by July 2011. Perhaps now the teething troubles were over and there was a reliable system that was compatible with the wheel.

Unfortunately, this was not to be. In October 2012 the cast iron shaft sheared through close to the coupling. BDC should have determined that the shaft was capable of withstanding the torque required to turn the gearbox. However, the company refused to accept any liability, claiming it was out of the one-year warranty.

The decision was taken to replace the shaft with a new mild steel one and the job was given to local steel fabricators TWS Ltd, at a cost of £19,920. This was completed in February 2013, about halfway through phase 2 of the restoration. Fortunately, the glass floor intended to allow viewing of the wheel from above had not been fitted, making access to the wheel chamber easier. The wheel was suspended and the flanges holding the spokes and paddles disconnected from the shaft. The shaft was extricated sideways out into the mill and then manoeuvred out of the building. This was done using a lifting frame and ratchets, and a lot of ingenuity. The original shaft now forms part of the display of old ironwork. The new shaft was then slid into place and two new roller bearings fitted. A coupling was placed between the shaft and gearbox to reduce the risk of shearing. Once again, after a lot of effort and expense, the wheel was turning and generating electricity. Despite the torque calculations being double checked and the new shaft x-rayed for any flaws after the flanges were welded to it, amazingly in October 2016, this shaft also sheared where the flange near to the gearbox was welded to it. Fortunately for RHT, the system was under warranty and yet another shaft, but of a design that should prevent the same problem occurring again, was fitted and turning two months later.

Other misfortunes have also occurred with the waterwheel system, most of which could be attributed to incompetence by so called professionals. Twice the generator has failed to be waterproof and needed re-winding. Following one of these, the wrong cog was fitted that subsequently caused damage to the gearbox. It then had to be lifted out and moved by hand-pushed trolley to the car park where it could be loaded on a truck and sent away for repair. Bearings in the generator have also had to be replaced twice. Each of these events not only incurred significant costs, but also resulted in lost generation and subsequent lost revenue for the trust.

Despite the many problems encountered with the wheel system, it is now able to deliver the expected 15 kW and runs quietly in the granary where it can be seen by visitors.

The second screw

At a meeting in September 2010, trustees agreed that RHT should start saving towards a deposit to install a second Archimedes Screw turbine. With a likely cost of £200,000 this seemed a daunting prospect. A loan for the bulk of this would be needed as by now there were no grants available towards the capital cost. The viability of the project would depend on the FiT payable on new hydro schemes. It was decided to approach the Charity Bank, an organisation set up to use funds from dormant accounts to provide loans to charities. After several meetings between Dave Mann, Chris Fawdington and a representative of the bank, it seemed likely that RHT through its trading arm the Howsham Power Company, would be offered a loan of £210,000 at 7.5% interest over 11 years. The cash flow forecast prepared by Dave showed that given the expected electricity generation and the FiT and sales income, this was financially viable. A formal application was submitted and all went quiet. Further information was sought by the bank and then a full valuation of the whole project was demanded, at RHT's expense. This was commissioned and the report finally produced in May 2016. Shortly after, the bank decided the loan no longer fitted their lending criteria and the application was rejected. More wasted time and money.

During 2016 a Polish company called Hydromew was interested in manufacturing and installing Archimedes Screw turbines in the UK. Dave went to the factory in Gdansk to evaluate their work. He also visited a couple of their projects in Poland. The company seemed capable of doing what it claimed and feedback from a private owner in the UK having an installation done by Hydromew was positive. The company put in a quote for manufacturing the screw, supplying a gearbox, generator and control panel, and completing all the civil works for around £140,000. This was a much lower quote than that from a western European equivalent and a contract was signed in September 2016. The capital would be provided by several private unsecured loans giving much greater flexibility in repayment.

A crew of four Polish workers arrived in late September to start preparing the sluice to receive the screw. They had brought an old caravan from another job they had been working on to live in while on site, thus keeping down costs. There was a language barrier to overcome and some dubious working practices, but soon the existing sluice wall had been removed and a concrete slab and walls to house the new screw were in place. The weather was favourable and the river level low allowing work to progress. At 4.4 m, it is slightly shorter than the first screw but with a greater diameter of 3 m, giving the screw twice the capacity, 4 cumec, and a potential output of 40 kW. It arrived on an articulated low loader that backed down into the car park, once a mobile crane was in position. Prior to its arrival, volunteers led by Paul Lister had spent many hours cutting back all the tree branches that had grown across the river since the last screw was delivered by pontoon ten years previously. The pontoon had been cleaned and repaired and an additional section added. Even so, when the crane lifted the screw and it could be weighed, it was found to be 10.5 t, one tonne more than expected, but fortunately still within the safe limit for the pontoon, so it was lifted on. The pontoon was sitting rather low in the water, but at least it was safely on board. If the screw had arrived a day earlier, as was the intention, the loaded pontoon would have fitted under the bridge. But it had been raining and the river level was going up. Getting the screw trapped under the bridge with a rising river was unthinkable, so moving it upstream was abandoned for the time being and the Polish staff left. It was not until two weeks later that they returned and by a combination of the two electric outboard motors, men pulling on attached ropes and pushing with scaffold poles, the screw was successfully delivered up the river. Over the next few days, the crew managed to pull the screw off the pontoon and roughly into position.

It was early May when Hydromew next returned to fit the new gates to both screws and put in one wide grill suspended from a new strong bridge allowing access to both screws. The men also excavated into the bed of the river so that the angle of the screw was correct to optimise electricity generation. This was only partially achieved. Once again, the Hydromew staff left with the vague promise that they would be back soon to finish the job. A further payment was made for the construction of the control panel to begin. This job was given to a Polish sub-contractor, Artur Wyrwas.

After three postponed return dates, a couple of men turned up in early August and stayed for two days. All this really achieved was to agree what still needed doing to complete the job. We were assured that a truck with the control panel would arrive on site on the 15th or 16th of the month, as well as Artur the installer. It was clear that Hydromew were struggling with a cash flow crisis, in part because of the approximately 20% fall in the value of sterling following the result of the Brexit referendum. At the trustees' meeting in September, it was agreed that we would propose to meet Hydromew halfway on this loss by offering an extra £11,000. Within days of agreeing this, RHT learnt that Hydromew had gone into liquidation.

The main item outstanding was the control panel. The angle of the screw was still not correct and the hydraulic system to raise the front of the screw when the river level was high and thus increase head and output, was missing. The gabion walls needed to be rebuilt to make them more secure. With the winter approaching and higher river levels, it was decided that the two latter items would have to wait until the following spring/summer to correct. Dave was in touch directly with Artur, who had a control panel built for the site and an obvious interest in fitting it and recouping his costs. Consequently, a deal was struck and we agreed to pay £12,000 for him to bring the panel to the UK, install it and commission the screw. There were other items to complete such as connecting up the hydraulics, fitting the generator to the gearbox, making the space around the screw safe with grating and completing the mesh cover over the blades of the screw. It became a bit like the installation of screw 1 with Dave and other trustees getting on and doing the work ourselves.

At the end of September Artur and his assistant arrived and started work. The equipment followed a few days later by truck from Poland. It was soon discovered that a vital part of the coupling between the gearbox and generator was missing. After searching for it both at another Hydromew site in the UK and at the factory in Poland, it became clear it had never been ordered. More delay and expense followed. Artur had to leave after he had done as much as he could, as without the generator fitted the system could not be tested and commissioned.

It was another month before Artur returned, during which time all the other problems had been resolved. While all the components seemed to work, something was not right. Eventually the problem was identified. The inverter, which Dave had acquired second-hand over one year earlier, needed an upgrade to the latest version of software. Once this had been installed, the second screw was finally generating. The output was modest in the initial tests at 25 kW at a lower than maximum speed. This was due to a number of possible reasons – debris in front of the screw affecting flow of water, the incorrect angle and a slight rubbing of the blades against the trough in one place. After testing, Artur left confident that the control system was working.

A few days later Dave tried increasing the speed of the screw to increase output. This meant more weight of water passing through the screw causing more force on the bearings. Something happened and an ominous noise developed. It sounded like large stones were passing through the screw. It was possible that stones in front of the gate were being dislodged with the increased flow, but the clunking sound remained when the speed was reduced. It soon became clear that the noise was coming from the lower bearing and its movement was irregular. When Dave was able to take the cover off the bearing, he found a few bits of broken steel. At least the bearing was full of grease and it was not our fault by running it dry. After sending photographs to what remained of Hydromew in Poland and talking with Ed Green, it seemed likely that there was damage to the roller bearings themselves. The prospect of yet more delay and expense lay ahead. Meanwhile all the good generating conditions of the last few months had been lost and interest payments on the loans were mounting, not to mention repayment of capital.

It was finally possible to remove the bearing on 22 December, when the river dropped just enough to expose the bolts. Dave still had to get in the river in his dry suit and work up to his neck in water. A digger lifted the 300 kg bearing out of position and it was taken to Ed Green's workshop for inspection. Ed said he did not have enough time to repair it, so we took up the offer to return it to Gdansk for free repair early in January. Once dismantled, it became apparent that while there was grease in it, water had also got in that prevented effective lubrication and caused the roller bearings to break up. This probably happened because the greasing pipes were left open and water penetrated once the river went up. Simply capping them could have prevented the damage, wasted time and expense.

Perhaps inevitably, the repair took longer than expected and it was the middle of February 2018 before the bearing was returned. A high river level and bad weather delayed fitting, which Dave partially achieved as the river was rising again on 5 March.

Other necessary remedial work was required, including welding bracing struts at the top of the frame, which was done by Ed Green. Once the bearing was in position it needed to be adjusted, which could only be done once the river level was significantly lower. Lastly, the water trapped inside the cylinder as a consequence of removing the bearing, had to be pumped out for which a new centrifugal pump was purchased. After much fiddling around trying different pipes and positions, this was achieved. The end of the screw in the river was not quite level and a hydraulic ram was brought in to raise one side a few centimetres. Ideally the end of the screw would have been lifted and the riverbed excavated further to get the angle of the screw correct and the end level. This could be done in the summer when the EA had finally decided, after an extended consultation and planning period, to install a fish pass in the weir adjacent to screw 1. The contractor had agreed to place a coffer dam right around the screws and the section of weir where the fish pass would go. This would dry out the area inside the dam making it much easier to excavate the riverbed. Work was due to start in the first week of June, but then the contractor and EA announced that it would all be postponed to 2019, as they did not think they would have enough time to complete before the river level went up in the autumn. In the event it was an exceptionally dry summer, ideally suited for working on the weir. The cost of the fish pass was then considered too high and ways of reducing it were being explored. As of end 2021, a decision to proceed with the construction had still not been made.

During the spring of 2018 a pair of grey wagtails decided to build a nest in the housing between the gearbox and generator. Before the screw could be run, we waited a few extra days until three chicks successfully fledged the nest. Then on Sunday 13 May the screw was started. Slowly at first and then allowing the variable speed of the gearbox and generator to increase until an output of 28 kW at a generator speed of 1500 rpm was achieved. There were no nasty noises, all was running smoothly. This was day one of the operation of the second screw and a proud moment in the continuing story of Howsham Mill. To date, the total cost of screw 2, including financing, has been £145,000, considerably less than originally forecast despite all the issues encountered. The loans and interest were paid off after only 30 months of operation. Some additional expenditure will be required to get the angle right and finish off the adjacent wall.

One idea conceived some years ago finally came to fruition in 2021. When installing the second screw, an insulated pipe was laid so that a connection could be made between coils in the gearboxes of both screws and the underfloor heating system. It took three attempts to find someone who was prepared and able to connect them up. The mixture of water and anti-freeze is now pumped through the coils at the base of the gearboxes, picking up some of the waste heat from friction in the oil, and flows to the pipes under the flagstone floor in the mill. This of course only operates when the screws are generating. The room temperature during the winter has been maintained at between 9 and 13 degrees, depending on the exterior temperature. This can then be supplemented with electric heaters and the wood stove to make the room comfortable for most activities.

In December 2021, a large cable was laid underground across the field to allow power to be delivered directly to Howsham Hall. This is sold at a price between the grid wholesale rate and the standard import rate, thus benefiting both Howsham Mill and Howsham Hall. It also nicely restores the historic connection between these two buildings, with the mill once again utilising the power of the River Derwent to benefit the Hall.

Performance over the first 12 years

We have endured many setbacks since the hydro-power scheme was first conceived. The systems have been delivering power consistently for 12 years now, exporting just over 2.25 million kWh of renewable electricity to the grid as of January 2022. The first figure shows the annual production in kWh over this period. This is only slightly less than that predicted by the original feasibility study, as shown in the second figure. The shortfall has been largely affected by the various problems described above, so there is good reason to be optimistic for the future.

The hydro-power scheme will continue to deliver green electricity for many years to come, which in turn provides the project with a reliable source of income to maintain the beautiful historic building, whilst continuing to provide valuable environmental education.

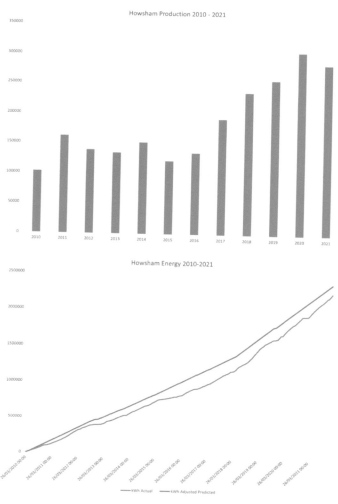

A mobile crane lifts screw 2 onto the pontoon February 2017
Photo: M Phillips

The two screws viewed from across the river 2018.
Photo: M Phillips.

Restoring the building

As the building emerged from years of neglect after the clearance of trees and shrubs, the scale of the restoration became clear. The whole building was without a roof. Although the remaining walls of the main part were largely intact, those of the single storey section to the west, which was to become known as the granary, were in a much worse state. The roof collapsed in the 1960s following a fire. Inevitably the walls then started to deteriorate as water got into the stone and brick work, weakening the mortar. Another problem was the ivy that had grown up the walls and was affecting the structure, and tree roots that were embedded in some sections of wall. With no immediate prospect of doing any major work to restore the building, stabilising the walls was the priority. To prevent further ingress of rainwater into the intact walls, a tarpaulin was laid along the tops.

Making a start

Initially the main effort was directed to the granary as this seemed the most likely part to start rebuilding and, being single storey, was easier to work on. The first of what were to become regular monthly volunteer workdays was on a Sunday in March 2005 when 32 people, young and old, came down with wheelbarrows, spades, saws and other tools. Just getting on the island was a challenge; you had to walk carefully over two steel girders laid across the canal where the new swing bridge is now located. Pushing a laden wheelbarrow along the girders was even more of a challenge.

Ivy was carefully pulled off the walls to minimise damage to the stones and crumbling mortar and then the roots were pulled up. Also growing into the walls were various trees and shrubs, some of which were firmly anchored within the masonry and took a considerable effort to remove. Two particularly large root balls embedded in the wall of the mill race had to be burnt to get rid of them. Bob 'the builder' Perkins of Ryedale Conservation Supplies provided lime mortar at £4 a bucket and tuition to those interested in learning about its use. By using it to point the stonework and cover the bare tops, the walls would be stabilised until such time as the full restoration could begin. One section of the granary that was saved from imminent collapse was the arch over the entrance to the mill race.

All the remaining pieces of ironwork and mill stones had to be removed from inside the building, some of which were heavy and awkward to lift and manoeuvre out. This was all done without special lifting equipment. There were pieces of the carved stonework from the roof that had fallen that might be usable in future. These were carefully lifted and put to one side. Bricks that had become dislodged from the walls were salvaged and the old mortar chiselled off so that later they could be reused. The other activity that started and would continue for many months to come, was the digging out of soil and silt that had accumulated over the years inside the building, in front of the wheel race and in the mill pond the other side. The only place to put all this material was to grade it on the island away from the building. Today it forms the slight mound where the shed is located, blending perfectly into the island. The excavation of the building was overseen by volunteer archaeologist Geraldine Mathieson from the Yorkshire Mills Group. While nothing of particular interest was found, a good collection of old bottles, clay pipes and other artefacts was unearthed. One important find was the foot of the original lead statue of Diana that had fallen into the wheel pit. Later, one of her forearms would be returned by the man who found it when he worked on repairs to the weir in the 1970s. He had read an article in the NFU magazine which described the discovery of Diana's foot. He drove from Oxford to return home the piece of Diana he had kept safe for so many years. The rest of the statue was probably taken for scrap and melted down.

These volunteer days became an enjoyable way to spend a Sunday. In the winter months someone would light a fire in which to cook jacket potatoes and brew tea over. At the end of the day people would leave tired in body, but with a sense of achievement; and a sense of the huge task ahead.

These activities provided volunteering opportunities for two groups in addition to individuals. Geoff Hutchison, a builder specialising in stonework, was also an organiser of people convicted of minor offences and given community service orders. He would bring a group down regularly on a weekend to do a variety of jobs, which later included helping him on the restoration of the granary. They had the chance to contribute to an interesting and innovative project in a beautiful location, more rewarding, for instance, than cleaning graffiti off walls. Some were also well qualified to advise on security measures for the lock-up storing the project's tools.

Young trainee soldiers in their first induction year at barracks near Harrogate were also regular volunteers. They were expected to complete the bronze medal of the Duke of Edinburgh's award and that required doing some appropriate voluntary work. The project provided such an opportunity and for several years, groups of up to 40 young men and women would descend on the island to help. Inevitably the groups varied in ability and enthusiasm; the best ones were led by NCOs who showed by example. Overall, they made a great contribution to the project, particularly where large numbers could tackle big jobs, such as digging the trench to lay the electricity cable across the field to the transformer.

Preparing the documents

Behind the scenes, Mo MacLeod was busy looking for funding from a variety of sources to start the restoration process. An initial grant from the Sustainable Development Fund administered through Yorkshire Forward was much less than expected, £8000 instead of £31,420. Crucially though, this paid for local joiner Geoff Norton to make the bridge that would go over the end of the lock where the gates were missing. This he made from green oak sourced locally in Hovingham. Laying the timber spars across the lock by sliding them along a ladder was a bit precarious, but once in the place the slats could be fitted and the bridge competed. At last, by late 2005 it was possible to get on the island without the risk of falling in the canal (as did happen) and heavier items could be brought down to the mill more easily. Other small grants were also obtained from various sources and a larger sum of money from the Howardian Hills AONB to start work on restoring the millrace, installing a sluice gate and constructing a new waterwheel.

Funding also allowed the production of architect's plans as part of an application to the planning department of Ryedale District Council. Andrew Yeats and his small team at Ecoarc, based in the next village of Harton, was the perfect choice as architect. As the name of his company suggests, he specialised in designing and adapting buildings to meet high standards of sustainability in material use and high levels of insulation to minimise energy consumption. By now the two main potential uses for the building had emerged. The first was as an education centre focussing on renewable energy and local history, to act as a resource centre and library. The second was as a bunkhouse for visitors arriving on foot, perhaps as part of a walking tour in the area. The two potential uses were not considered mutually exclusive and provided a brief for Ecoarc.

The plans that Andrew produced were not that different from what is in place today. The granary would be a kitchen with a compost toilet and cabinet for all the electrical equipment. The main part of the mill would be a teaching/meeting area downstairs with a mezzanine first floor for a library and bunkhouse. The void in the floor was to retain the beautiful tall window on the east façade, allowing light to penetrate both levels. Linking the granary and the main part of the mill would be a glass covered floor over the wheel. New windows, including opening up the blind window in the south façade, and new doors on the north and south sides were included. A spiral staircase would provide access to the upper level.

Also under preparation during 2005 was a feasibility study for the whole project. It was published in April 2006 and presented the background and history of the mill, the conservation philosophy of the project, the potential for hydro-electricity generation, possible uses for the building and their associated advantages and disadvantages, costs and potential income. A crucial contribution was the report of the structural engineer, Mr DAC Wood. He concluded that while the building had suffered from ingress of water damaging the upper courses, damage from tree roots, some settlement and a severe lack of maintenance, the walls were structurally sound and once repaired, they would support a first floor and a new pyramidal roof. He also thought that the granary could be repaired along with the wheel sluice and a new wheel put in place. With this assurance, using the plans prepared by Ecoarc and preliminary costs provided by quantity surveyors Turner and Holman of York, an initial budget was drawn up. This budget then needed to be matched with funds from suitable donors in order to achieve the goal of restoring the neglected building back to its former glory.

The feasibility study listed sixteen sources of income already going into the project, from £500 donated by the East Yorkshire Georgian Society to £50,000 from the DTI Clear Skies fund. But much more would be needed; £790,000 was the initial estimate for both the building restoration and the hydro scheme. The Heritage Lottery Fund (HLF) was identified early on as a potential donor. Following a visit by an officer from HLF, he encouraged RHT to put in a grant application.

The preferred scheme that emerged in the feasibility study was in three phases. The first was the restoration of the single storey extension to the west known as the granary, including the wheel chamber and reinstatement of the wheel to generate electricity. The second phase was renovation of the basic structure of the main part of the building to make it usable, and installation of two Archimedes Screw turbines. The third phase would be the restoration of the stonework on the outside of the building. This phasing was to allow for gradual attraction of funds, demonstrating to donors what RHT could achieve. In practice things worked out differently.

Getting planning permission

Before any work could start on the building, other than the stabilisation, RHT needed to get planning approval for the work, and as it is a Grade 11 listed building, listed buildings approval. After two years of work all the plans and documentation were submitted to the council. The response from the planning officer was not positive. Although RHT had submitted several letters of support and there was only one spurious objection from the then owner of the adjacent fields, the planning officer thought the building too far gone for a small band of well-meaning enthusiasts to restore. RHT was advised that it should be content with keeping the mill as a 'managed ruin'. He also raised the issue of car parking. This was a genuine concern as there is only a small area of public space by the bridge where the different river users could park safely off the road. Sir Fred, RHT's patron, came to the rescue by offering a piece of land by the bridge next to the river that could be cleared and a stone surface laid to accommodate sufficient cars. Thus, on 17 January 2006, it was with some trepidation that trustees and supporters gathered at the RDC planning committee meeting where the application was to be heard. Andrew Yeats, the architect, spoke authoritatively about the merits of the project. Val Hood, supporter and soon to be trustee, spoke about the great benefits she saw, as a retried science teacher, for the restored building as an education centre. The planning officer spoke of all the negatives she saw about the project. It was then the turn of councillors to comment on the application. Imagine the delight of the supporters when the first councillor to speak thought it a 'brilliant' project – restoring a beautiful building, public involvement, environmental education, renewable electricity generation. The next to speak said 'it was just the sort of project we should be supporting'. When the vote came, the recommendation of the planning officer was rejected and councillors voted unanimously to approve the planning application. There was a list of conditions to meet, including provision of a car park, but nothing insurmountable. Now at last the trustees and supporters could see the real possibility of the project succeeding. They could also see the long road ahead to realise that goal.

In contrast to the planning officer, the listed buildings officer, Emma Woodland, was supportive of the restoration of the building. Throughout the process of agreeing the final plans and specifications she was constructive and helpful in achieving a restored building that was faithful to the original design, using appropriate materials and methods, yet was fit for the 21st century and beyond.

Phase 1

Having secured planning permission and agreed a phased programme for the project, firm commitments for funding needed to be secured. An application to the Rural Enterprise Scheme (RES) was prepared with the help of a consultant, for the restoration of the granary to provide a kitchen, a simple compost toilet and facilities for housing generation equipment for the hydro systems. It was a European Union funded scheme administered by Defra, the Department for Food and Rural Affairs. Applications for this grant were typically for farm building conversions for other activities on farms, but the restoration of buildings in rural areas for community use also came under its remit. The unusual nature of RHT's application may have been to its advantage. The application was submitted in time to be considered at the June 2006 panel meeting. The application was successful. RHT was awarded a grant of £108,651 towards the total cost, which required RHT to raise £30,000 of match funding.

Restoration Village

During 2006, Mo MacLeod heard about the Restoration Village programme made by the BBC and hosted by Griff Rhys Jones. In previous years, this programme had showcased different projects seeking funds for restoring buildings. It gave the viewing public the opportunity to vote for the one they thought most worthy. Howsham Mill seemed to fit the criteria for inclusion in the proposed programme that year and Mo submitted an application. She knew that this could be a game changer, as the winner would get all the money needed to complete their project. When she heard that the project had been chosen to take part, all the stops were pulled out to generate publicity for the mill. To win needed the votes of the public, so the public had to know about the project and be convinced it should be the winner. There followed a series of press interviews, putting up posters all around the area, handing out leaflets, making banners, printing T-shirts - anything that would link Howsham Mill with the programme. A major open day was organised for Sunday 10 September. The bus company, Yorkshire Coastliner, kindly laid on a special bus service doing a loop from Malton to the mill and back. This not only solved the parking problem likely at Howsham Bridge if the numbers anticipated came by car, but also added to publicity and the green credentials of the project. A group of supporters of the mill set up some stalls in Malton marketplace talking about the project and encouraging people to take the free bus ride out to Howsham. The day was a great success, with about 500 people visiting the mill in one day, all without any congestion on the roads or on the island.

In August, the production team spent one Sunday at the mill with a camera crew filming the piece about the project that would be broadcast on 8 September, two days before the open day. The two experts who were introducing and describing all the nominated buildings, Ptolemy Dean and Marianne Suhr, came upon the mill with no prior knowledge of what to expect and their reactions to the building were filmed. Griff Rhys Jones, the host of the show, was also there, getting stuck in by digging silt out from the mill race. Two old men who knew it as a working mill when they were young, were brought down for the first time in many years. They were delighted to be part of the day and their pleasure was recorded. The mill was one of four projects in the northern region featured and for which the public could vote. When the votes were counted, Howsham Mill was the winner of the northern heat. This meant that representatives could go to the live final to be held at the Down and Weald Museum near Chichester.

Early on Sunday morning 17 September a coach paid for by the BBC left Westow with trustees and supporters headed for the south coast. The programme went out live that evening, with representatives of the regional winners seated in what was a replica of an Elizabethan theatre. Mo MacLeod did a relaxed and informative interview with Griff Rhys Jones and clips of the sequence filmed at the mill were shown. After all the projects had been presented, there was a nerve wracking wait while the votes were counted. Despite the mill getting around 27,000 votes, the winner was Chedham's Yard, an old tool shed in Warwickshire, a much less interesting building than Howsham Mill, but with a fantastic historic collection of tools. It was a great event to be part of and brought much publicity to the project. Nearly three years later, when the winning project had received all the funds it needed, what was left over was distributed to other worthy participants. Two trustees of the restoration fund visited the mill and described the project as 'magical', offering RHT a grant of £50,000.

With the RES grant secured, work could begin on the granary in 2007. Geoff Hutchinson took on the job of stonemason for the build, with weekend help from community service volunteers. Another builder, John Adams, had introduced himself as a 'former vandal'; he had come to the island as a young man to fish and had contributed to the demise of the abandoned building. Now he wanted to make amends and he and his assistant were the brickie and general builder for the project. Geoff Norton made and installed the timber spars for the new roof. Mel Fox, who was later to become a trustee, was taken on as the part-time project administrator.

Existing stone and bricks were cleaned up and used where possible, though new stone was brought in and several thousand bricks from a reclamation yard. Ted Pindar, a retired builder who used to work on the Duncombe Estate at Helmsley, spent many hours dressing stone for the walls. In one corner a steel cabinet was installed that would house the electrical control equipment. Work progressed well until mid-summer when heavy and prolonged rain brought the river level up, inundating first the footpath to the island and then the mill. This was to be the first of several floods that would cover part of the island and the building. No damage was caused, but work was not possible for more than two weeks.

As the roof spars were put in place, funds began to run low and an urgent 'raise the roof' appeal was launched, asking members of the public to buy 1500 slates at £2 each. The response was magnificent, raising £3499 and the roof was finished. The floor of reclaimed flagstones laid over electric heating mats, was set at a slight fall to allow water to drain out of the building. Windows and a stable-type door were handmade from hardwood at some expense but designed to match the period of the building. Inside an electrician installed the necessary lighting and sockets, while volunteers plumbed in a reclaimed Belfast sink and a rainwater harvesting system. This consists of a 2500 gal tank filled by water collected off the roof via the gutter. The water is pumped through two particulate filters into a header tank. This feeds cold taps via a UV filter to kill any bacteria or the large hot water tank, which supplies water to the hot taps, again passing through a UV filter. Later a solar thermal panel was fitted on the south facing roof to heat water in the tank. With no mains water, a wheelchair-accessible compost toilet was constructed next to the steel cabinet. A fridge and electric cooker were installed, above flood level, and rather cheap but functional worktops. These were replaced in 2013 with custom made units using wood from an ash tree that blew down on the island. It had a good stem, which after much effort was manhandled off the island, taken to a wood yard to be planked and then turned into the finished worktops, shelves and drawers. In a small way, this exemplifies the ethos of the project – using available natural materials, crafted with care by local labour, and as with so much of the project, 'doing it the hard way'.

At the same time, the wall next to the millpond was repaired. This was in worse condition than originally thought and consequently took much longer to rebuild than expected, and costs escalated. A private short-term loan helped get this work finished. The grant from the Restoration Village fund was timely in allowing this loan to be repaid.

With the completion of the phase 1 construction by the end of 2007 and the progress made on the hydro installation, there was a feeling that the project was really underway. But this good feeling received a severe jolt just a few months later. One of the trustees was shocked to find that vandals had thrown rocks through all the windows, smashing not only the glass but also severely damaging the frames. One or more of the vandals got inside and trashed the place, breaking and destroying whatever they could. It was a depressing realisation that there were people who would come to an idyllic location and then try and destroy all the hard work done by so many. This was the first of three major thefts or incidents of vandalism experienced during the restoration. In order to prevent future break-ins, tough Perspex sheets were fitted to the repaired windows and a security gate installed in front of the granary door. In 2011 the solar thermal panel was stolen off the

With the trees and undergrowth cleared, the scale of the restoration becomes clear 2005.

Ted Pindar, John Adams and Geoff Hutchinson working on the granary 2007.
Photo: M Phillips.

roof. This was a planned theft for the panel itself as the pipe fitting had been carefully disconnected and the heavy and unwieldy panel carried back to the road. These events and other less serious vandalism were setbacks that made the trustees and supporters all the more determined to finish the job.

Phase 2

With the encouragement of the HLF representative who visited the mill, Mo MacLeod started on the long process of applying for a grant for the complete restoration of the main part of the building. This would be in two stages. The first was an application for a grant to prepare all the documentation needed for a full application. This required a complete set of architect's drawings, detailed specifications for all the work, a fully costed budget, a conservation architect's report on the history of the building and its future conservation, and a report from an education consultant on the potential uses of the finished building for teaching and learning. A grant for £19,500 was awarded by HLF to RHT, and with match funding from the Country Houses Foundation (CHF) and income from electricity sales, the target of £39,500 was reached. The team of professionals given the work included the same architect who had already done the preliminary plans, Andrew Yeats

The horse and cart bringing new stone for the mill to the site.
Photo: M Phillips.

Putting the roof hip beams together required ingenuity and many hands.
Photo: M Phillips.

of Ecoarc, David Fothergill from quantity surveyors Turner and Holman of York, and structural engineer Gez Pegram of Alan Young Partners, also in York. The conservation management plan was prepared by Edmund Simons of consultants Mouchel and the Learning and Activity Plan was produced by education consultants John Gorton and Nick Geen.

Once all the documents were drafted and agreed with the trustees, more work was required in checking through the budget and doing the finishing touches to the final presentation. Applications that get through the first stage are not always approved at the second stage; trustees were not complacent that the grant would be approved at the first attempt. When Mo received a letter from the head of HLF in Yorkshire and Humber in October 2011, she opened it with some trepidation. But the news was good. The HLF was awarding RHT a grant of £643,100, 82% of the total budget submitted. The money was for the restoration of the mill, improvements to the granary and three years of education provision. The other 18% was coming from the Country Houses Foundation, income from electricity sales, a promise from a private donor of £10,000 and the value of volunteer time put into the restoration.

It was important that RHT found the right contractor for the job. Six tenders were required by HLF. Representatives of the companies all visited the site early in 2012. This gave the trustees the opportunity to assess those likely to be involved in the work as it was clear that both parties needed to be able to work together effectively. All the companies were from within about 20 miles of the mill. Not all the work could be done by the smaller contractors and items such as joinery, roofing and electrical were sub-contracted, but with the main contractor responsible for all the co-ordination. Once all the tenders were in, they were reviewed by Gez Pegram, who was acting as project manager, quantity surveyor David Fothergill, and Mo MacLeod and Martin Phillips as clients. The six companies were then invited to an interview with the above to allow questioning on the detail of their tenders. It became clear that the contractor offering the lowest tender did not have sufficient experience in the traditional techniques required. The tenders were then scored for price, value for money and ability to undertake the work. At the end of the process the unanimous choice was Stephen Pickering Ltd, a small company specialising in traditional building work and based near Kirbymoorside. He had included Houghtons of York as the joinery sub-contractor, a company well-suited for the work, and Listers of York as the electrical sub-contractor, also a company with a good reputation. The HLF project officer accepted this choice of main contractor. Martin was able to take on the role of site manager and this proved invaluable. Despite all the plans and specifications, practical decisions needed to be made on-site with Stephen much more frequently than the scheduled monthly meetings with the structural engineer and the architect.

A delay arose with the need for legal work to extend the lease on the car park and for the HLF to hold a charge over the mill and island. Once this was done and Stephen Pickering could mobilise, work finally started on Monday 11 June 2012. The first few days were taken up by getting the scaffolding onto the island. Negotiating access across the field for heavy items with the landowner had proved difficult. He didn't like the idea of vehicles being used but didn't object to horse-drawn transport. To allow wider access to the island, a scaffolding bridge was erected across the canal where the swing bridge once stood. A horse and cart, normally used for transporting logs out of sensitive woodland, was hired with its driver. They would return later to bring stone and other heavy items across the field.

The first big decision to make was the choice of stone for all the new carved work on the roof and for repairing the walls where necessary. Stone samples from two quarries in north-east England and one in Sussex were acquired and all interested parties met to compare them and make a choice. The two samples from the nearer quarries were a sandstone that would not be entirely compatible with the existing stone. The stone from Lamb's quarry in Sussex was an oolitic limestone, part of the same geological seam from which the original stone had been quarried nearby, probably at Birdsall. The only problem was the price; considerably more expensive than had been budgeted for. The building industry was still in a bit of a recession, the quarry wanted what was a large and valuable order and thus a deal was struck. There were a few pieces of Hildenley limestone, which had been used to make repairs to the building in the past, which needed replacing. This stone came from a quarry to the west of Malton, the only one in the country and long abandoned; a close match was the white Chicksgrove limestone. All the detailed carving of the stone for the crocketed finials, the pedestals and the dormer windows would be done at the quarry using a set of drawings prepared by the architect based on the old photograph of the mill in 1950 and the remaining pieces of stonework. These drawings were turned into a computer program that guided a circular saw to cut the stone. The final dressing of the stone, the stonemason's markings, was done on-site by Stephen Pickering.

Joiners from Houghtons came and started to make templates for doors and windows and to design the roof wall plate and hip beams. The electrician came to discuss how to wire the building without spoiling it. Copper MICC cable was chosen that would fix onto the walls to avoid cutting into the brick. A lighting design was agreed. There would be wall-mounted LED lights downstairs for a subtle effect, with overhead panels when more light was needed. Upstairs, LED units would be fitted within the spars and purlins. Conduits hidden within the first floor and behind the ceiling panels would house the cables. Sockets downstairs would be fitted well above the peak flood level.

Meanwhile the upper courses of brick and stone needed to be rebuilt and tied together to take the weight of the new roof. The joints of the walls both inside and out needed to be raked out and repointed with specially prepared lime mortar. The blind window on the south elevation was cut out and the arch rebuilt. The first delivery of stone was on 14 August and the horse and cart returned to bring it to the island. This included the string course for the top of the walls. Each large rectangle of stone was lifted by block and tackle up a scaffolding tower put up on the east side. The stone blocks were moved around the scaffolding walkway on a small trolley and then lifted into position by hand. Once this course was complete, the timber wall plate, four beams laid on the top of the walls and tied together by stainless steel braces, could be fitted. This required a team of twelve men. It was not until early

Stephen Pickering assembling one of the crocketed finials.
Photo: M Phillips.

October that the four hip beams could be fitted, each slotting into a wooden boss in the apex of the roof. Once again installation needed a large gang of men under the supervision of Stephen Pickering, who had carefully thought through how the operation would proceed. Houghtons had earlier assembled the roof hip beams and purlins in their yard to make sure it all fitted. Once the first beam was in position, the other three followed relatively quickly.

The next big lift was of the 8.5 m long oak beams weighing up to 1000 kg that were to hold up the first floor. For this a mechanical digger was brought in to lift each beam onto a scaffold frame, the only time it was on the island. The beam was sat on rollers so that it could be pushed through a hole cut into the north wall, onto another frame and into a recess made in the south wall.

At the end of September the island was partially flooded, necessitating a pause in the work, but the river soon went down and activity could restart. Then disaster struck. The waterwheel shaft suddenly and dramatically sheared. There was no alternative but to get it out and replace it with a new one. It had to be carefully and skilfully manoeuvred sideways into the mill and then out of the building while construction work carried on. November was turning into a wet month. Materials for the floor were brought down, including the Leca insulation in large bags. Flagstones reclaimed from an old woollen mill in West

The mill surrounded by water in the flood of January 2021.
Photo: M Phillips.

Diana lit up at night.
Photo: M Phillips.

Yorkshire were due to be delivered but conditions were too wet and getting worse. On 28 November the river gauge at Buttercrambe reached 2.38 m, not far off the highest level of 2.57 m recorded in November 2000. Little work was possible until the following January due to further flooding and the Christmas break.

A subsequent spell of sub-zero temperatures meant only work inside the building was possible. Even then doors and windows had to be boarded up and portable heating installed. Finally it was safe to lay the new floor in two stages. The first consisted of a base of hardcore, then a layer of the Leca insulation material and a slab

Setting up for the Christmas Fair upstairs in the mill 2014. The roof lights and dormer windows allow in plenty of natural light.
Photo: M Phillips.

of calcrete (lime and aggregate mix). The second half of the operation was done once the calcrete had set. A membrane was laid on which the heating pipe was fitted in a coiled pattern that would connect in with the hot water tank in the granary. Another layer of calcrete was then poured on top of the pipes. Finally, the flagstones were laid with a slight fall to the south so that flood water would drain out of the three original, but modified, drainage points in the wall.

The final fourth flood was at the end of January preventing work for about one week. Once the river went down, work restarted in earnest. The roof was slated with Burlington slates, more work could then be done on the ornate dormer windows and finials, a brick chimney was built and lined, and connected to a wood burning stove. Once the stonework was completed, the detailed lead flashing could be installed. The electrical fit progressed well, floorboards were laid and a staircase constructed. The original idea of a spiral staircase had been dropped. While this was all going on the new waterwheel shaft had to be fitted. This required new bearings mounted on specially made concrete pads, the only place in the building where cement was used.

The windows and doors made off-site were brought to the mill and fitted. Reluctantly, due to previous vandalism of the granary windows, Perspex sheets were fitted to the outside and discreet security bars on the inside. Before the scaffolding came down, the new statute of Diana had to be installed on the apex of the roof. Some weeks earlier, Martin had been in touch with Nikki Taylor a sculptor working with stainless steel mesh. Looking at examples of her work on her website, this material looked ideal for a roof sculpture – light, durable, and in contrast to a lead figure, unlikely to be stolen. She kindly agreed to design and make a statue of Diana at cost price. The exquisite detail of her can only be fully appreciated close up, or from the ground through binoculars. A plywood plinth covered in lead was made by the roofer, with holes drilled to Nikki's specification. Diana was then carried up and bolted to the plinth. Installing her on 12 April was not quite the topping off ceremony. There was still work to be done finishing the joinery and electrics, laying cobbles immediately around the building, and fitting glass floors over the wheel and the wheel pit once the new shaft was installed and the wheel operating again. Fire alarm and intruder alarm systems were fitted.

Another contractor was brought in to enlarge and lay a stone surface over the car park, including a tarmac connection with the road as demanded by the Highways Authority. They also laid a hard surface footpath as far as the lock bridge.

Almost exactly one year after starting and about nine weeks later than expected, the restoration was complete – well almost. Building control insisted on another emergency light, there were small snags to sort and there were the worktops in the granary to make. The latter took several months and were made by Stephen Drake, who worked on the restoration. The effort put into these worktops epitomised the effort, pride and craftsmanship that went into the whole restoration. Everybody, the professional design team (with one exception), all of Stephen Pickering's staff and the sub-contractors who worked on the project, put great effort and care into their work and can be rightly proud of their contribution to the restoration of this beautiful building. Like most complex building projects, things did not always go to plan. It was the flexibility and desire of all those involved to do a good job that meant solutions were always found to the many problems encountered along the way.

The quality of the restoration is reflected in the awards it has won. In 2013, the York Guild of Building presented their annual award to Stephen Pickering and his team. Also in that year the project won the Ryedale Rural Awards green project. In November 2014, Howsham Mill was one of the contenders for the national Heritage Angel Award organised by English Heritage in the category, best restoration of an industrial building. Five trustees attended the event held in London at a West End theatre. After a tense time sitting through some entertainment and the short video presentations prepared for the contenders, Howsham Mill was named as winner. The next month two trustees were back in London to receive, jointly with another project, the Heritage Hero award from the Heritage Alliance. This was closely followed by a highly commended award from The Georgian Society, again at a ceremony in London.

Since the restoration was completed there have been two major floods. The first in December 2015 and again in January 2021, as well as some minor flooding. There is sufficient warning of a flood to allow items to be moved above the likely water level to minimise damage and disruption. The building has proved to be resilient and once the water has receded there has been no significant damage. The main consequence is a layer of silt left behind on the floor. Water is pumped from the river and the silt is flushed out of the building and the floors brushed down. Paint work and other surfaces are easily cleaned. While water gets into the lime mortar of the walls, unlike with cement mortar, it can easily escape and the building will dry out in a few weeks.

One feature that was not included in the restoration was a replacement sundial. A photograph taken in the 1960s of the south elevation shows a sundial on a ledge above the door. It disappeared sometime after and was presumably the rather sinister looking one mentioned in the newspaper article of 1926, described in the history chapter. To remedy this omission, Jennifer Tetlow, a local stone carver, was commissioned to make a new one using a piece of stone from the island. It was put in place on the ledge above the south door in November 2021 and correctly indicates the time (GMT) when the sun is shining.

The completed mill from the south.
Photo: M Phillips.

The swing bridge

When it was a working corn mill, access to the island was across a timber swing bridge that spanned the canal. It can just be seen in a recently discovered photograph taken in 1974 and, anecdotally, some of it was still present in the 1980s, but no trace of it remained by 2003. In its place were two steel girders, just sufficient to walk across. In the early discussions with HLF, the possibility of restoring the stone piers and putting in a new bridge was discussed. Trustees could already see how useful vehicle access would be, not for regular use but to get heavy items on and off the island. But the HLF project officer advised against including the bridge in the application. When the final cost of the phase 2 restoration was added up, it came to

The new swing bridge over the canal.
Photo: M Phillips.

£420,000. Once the continuing education costs and other likely expenditure until December 2015 were accounted for, it was clear that there were sufficient funds remaining from the total grant offered by HLF to pay for a new bridge. The proposal was put to HLF and they agreed we could use the surplus money for that purpose. RHT would still have to find the 18% match funding. When trustees from the Country Houses Foundation were visiting to see the completed building restoration they had helped fund, they were so impressed with what had been achieved that they offered a second grant to cover the match funding required for the bridge.

The initial idea was that it would be a timber bridge, like the original. No photographs of it had come to light in time on which to base the design. A print dating from the mid-19th century of a technical drawing for a swing bridge over the Kennett and Avon canal was found and this looked appropriate for the one at Howsham. The original pintle or pivot on which the bridge rotated was still in place, but the structural engineer consulted did not think it capable of taking the sort of weight needed if the bridge was to have practical use. The design then evolved to a new pintle with a galvanised steel frame and oak decking and rails. From a distance it would appear to be a timber bridge. Planning permission and listed buildings approval were again required. As part of the consultation, RHT had to demonstrate to the EA that it posed no additional flooding risk and to NE that otters and other wildlife would be unaffected.

Eventually all the necessary permissions were obtained and two quotes received. The total cost of the quote from the preferred companies was £88,300. Stephen Pickering did the repairs necessary to the stone piers on either side of the canal; the pintle and frame were made and fitted by TWS Ltd, the local firm that had replaced the waterwheel shaft; the oak cladding was all prepared off-site by Yorkshire Oak Frames Ltd, based near Harrogate. The clock was ticking down to the deadline for submitting the final claim to HLF in time to be paid by 31 December 2015. The pintle and frame were installed on 21 November allowing the joiners to move in and lay the base and bolt on the rails a week or so later. The pintle is not in the centre of the bridge so the weight on both sides has to balance exactly by fitting steel weights, otherwise it would be impossible to swing. Naturally, there was some apprehension when it was first swung, which it did perfectly. The result is a bridge that looks as though it has always been there - the right design and beautifully crafted. Indeed, it looks similar to the original shown in the photograph that has recently come to light. Visitors often ask, why bother to make it a swing bridge when there is no longer boat traffic along the canal? The answer, of course, is that as it used to be a swing bridge, it was right to replace it with a new one.

New uses for an old mill

Unless Howsham Mill was to become just the most beautiful power station in the country, new uses needed to be found for it. Following initial meetings with residents of Howsham and surrounding villages, there was potential for the mill to become a community meeting place. This was always a rather vague idea, but with no village hall in Howsham, there was the occasional need for a place to hold meetings. Another early idea was making the mill a bunk house. The canoe clubs using the weir and river for their activities expressed interest in using the building for accommodation. They thought it would allow them to run training camps from the island. Discussions with a representative of the Youth Hostels Association (YHA) identified the mill as an ideal bunk house, forming part of the YHA's Green Beacon network of eco-friendly, carbon neutral accommodation. It was thought that the mill could accommodate up to fourteen overnight visitors, with an estimate of 230 stays per year and a potential annual income of £2300.

While fourteen people might be able to bed down for the night on the first floor of the mill, little thought was given to how they would all cook for themselves in the limited space in the granary, or to washing and toilet facilities. And how would the visitors be organised? Would they be trusted to collect a key from somewhere nearby, or would a warden be required to stay over when there were visitors? Although this proposal was approved as one of the permitted uses in the planning permission for the restored mill, it soon became apparent that it was going to be too complicated and too demanding for RHT to manage, at least in the first few years after restoration, and has never been implemented.

Also considered in the early stages of the project were visits to the mill and island by school groups. An education pack was prepared that was sent out to local schools. The response from them was positive with supportive letters received from the head teachers of nearby Langton and Leavening primary schools. School visits later became part of the HLF bid and comprehensive education proposals were developed.

Another early proposal was to run craft courses inside the building or outside on the island. In fact, these started well before building work commenced. With funding from the Local Heritage Initiative, Angela Coles and Geoff Norton of Yorkshire Hurdles were commissioned to put on a series of courses from October 2005 to June 2006 including three-legged stool making, natural Christmas decorations, making willow figures and structures, and green wood working. Some of the latter courses resulted in an oak table with benches and two further benches, still on the island. Over the years all ages have enjoyed subsidised courses covering mosaics, stone carving, wood turning, making wire figures, jewellery making, willow weaving, painting and drawing, making Christmas decorations and bushcraft.

Before the main part of the restoration started, there were two open air screenings in the roofless building that attracted good audiences, partly for the novelty of the first hydro-powered outdoor cinema in the country. The first one even attracted a film crew from Channel 4 to feature it on an arts programme. These were part of the Screenwaves programme in North Yorkshire. In 2015 the mill became a venue showing films under the banner of Cine North, bringing cinema to rural locations, this time indoors. Screenings continued in subsequent years during the spring to autumn period, when the weather is better and days longer. Venturing down to the mill at night in the winter is not a particularly attractive proposition, whereas on a warm, sunny summer's evening, having a picnic or drink before a film show in a beautiful and unusual location, makes for a special evening out. The attendance has been variable, ranging from sold out to just a few patrons. The choice of film is critical and getting that right has not been easy.

Educational visits

The intention was always to use the building for as many activities as possible and particularly for education. As part of the HLF grant, three years' funding for an education and events officer was provided together with materials needed to equip and promote the mill. The first incumbent to the post was Liz Vowles, who started on 1 October 2012 working three days per week. Her initial task was to re-write the activity plan, which was accepted by HLF in March 2013. It set out the courses, school visits, events and other activities proposed for the next three years, to be modified in the light of experience. She worked with a local company to develop a new website and a computer animation of the original internal workings of the mill when grinding corn. Looking through the proposed list of activities in hindsight, all but one of them was tried. Some were not popular or did not work, while the more successful ones have been repeated.

Liz left in August 2013 to take up a teaching post. She was replaced by Jen Wakefield who started in November of that year. This coincided with the completion of the restoration of the building so that it could be used by visiting groups. Jen was able to take advantage of contacts made with schools, the Yorkshire Wildlife Trust and Howardian Hills AONB. This collaboration resulted in the mill hosting joint visits by rural primary schools in Ryedale with urban primary schools in York and Hull, in a school twinning project. The two visiting schools chose either a renewable energy theme or a bread-making theme. Both courses allowed the children to learn how the mill worked in the past and how it works today and to participate in a practical activity. There were twelve schools involved that brought about 350 pupils over six days. It was clear from talking to pupils and teachers at the end of the visits and from feedback collected from teachers subsequently, that the days were successful in showing the pupils renewable energy generation first-hand and allowing them to build models of waterwheels or to make bread. However, attracting school groups to visit has been more difficult than anticipated. Teachers have a choice of venues to which they can take pupils, and the cost of transport is a major consideration for any school trip. To meet these challenges, visits to the mill were designed to cover aspects of key stages in the primary school curriculum, notes were prepared for teachers and in some cases transport costs were subsidised.

The health and safety of children during their visits was obviously a key priority from the start. Some schools thought that the proximity of the river made the site inherently too risky for young children. There was never any intention of permanently fencing off the river. The education officer carefully thought through all the potential risks and how to respond to them, coming up with risk assessments for different age groups. One schools visit officer for North Yorkshire County Council considered these inadequate and suspended visits from schools in the county. RHT employed a H&S consultant to prepare a H&S Management System to remedy this before school visits were able to recommence.

Helen Spring, a qualified teacher, took over the education remit in September 2015. She developed her own courses to meet the changing requirements of the National Curriculum for primary schools. The wheel and screws offer practical examples to learn about gears, levers and pulleys. The children have then been given an opportunity to make model gearing systems using craft materials. The generators provide a backdrop to explain what electricity is and how it is produced, and specifically about renewable sources. Some groups have made solar ovens, and models of waterwheels and wind turbines. RHT purchased some data loggers, expensive items that many schools do not own. These can be used for their pupils' investigations to answer such questions as 'how hot does my solar oven get?', 'how noisy is an Archimedes Screw turbine when operating?' or 'what happens to the brightness of the sun over the course of a day?'

A craft course making wire figures held downstairs inside the mill.
Photo: M Phillips.

Helen used the site to gain her qualification in forest school teaching. Essentially, this is all about children exploring and learning about the countryside, what lives and grows there and how to do things such a make a fire, prepare dough and cook unleavened bread over the embers, and to construct a simple shelter. These are activities universally enjoyed by children, but which many have never tried before. As the island is part of the SSSI, the place provides an excellent opportunity to learn about habitats, and the plants and animals that live on and around the island. A range of age-appropriate activities has been developed. These include identifying mini beasts, making bug 'caravans', creating classification keys and writing a 'habitat postcard', which helps children to begin to describe different habitats. The original function of the mill leads into the production of wheat, grinding the grain into flour and making bread. These can be linked to design and technology objectives. The children all have a tour over the mill and can see for themselves the old machinery retained from its milling days and the new machinery for the generation of electricity. Even the compost toilets have an educational function. Children, and some of the accompanying adults, have no idea that at least half the children in the world only have use of such a toilet.

Feedback from both children and teachers has been collected since starting the programme. It is clear from their reactions that the children enjoy their visits; a common highlight is cooking marshmallows over the fire. The teachers have been asked to email in a feedback form and the responses have always been positive and any suggestions for improvement constructive. The comments from one teacher sum up the feedback Helen has received: *We loved every activity during our day and the amount of learning throughout each one was outstanding. The children were thoroughly engaged and enjoyed everything. They did not even want to stop for lunch! Helen has so much knowledge and is personable, inspiring and creative.*

Since the start of the project until summer 2021, a total of about 3800 pupils from 34 schools and two home-schooled groups have come to the mill for an organised visit. These have mostly been primary school pupils for whom the subjects seem more appropriate than for secondary school pupils. Helen has provided regular sessions for home-schooled primary age children, giving them an opportunity to mix with their peers and do outdoor

The first hydro-powered outdoor cinema in the country May 2011.
Photo: T Bartholomew.

School children sitting around the fire.
Photo: M Phillips.

activities. In addition, another tutor has run practical outdoor sessions for older home-schooled children.

The Covid-19 pandemic which started in spring 2020 and continued in 2021, seriously curtailed educational activities and other events. School visits restarted in the summer term of 2021 and proved very popular as most of the activities took place outdoors.

The mill and island have also afforded college and university students studying a range of courses a valuable field visit. Students from Bishop Burton College, Askham Bryan College, Kirklees College, Selby College, York College and the University of York have all made visits relevant to courses they are pursuing. These have included building construction, public service, environmental studies, fisheries, heritage conservation and even art and design. Groups of students on canoeing trips down the river have camped overnight on the island, experiencing what it is like to be self-sufficient, cooking over an open fire, washing in the river and sleeping in a tent.

During 2014, the mill was the base of the local Norton Wildlife Watch group. Several joint events with the group were held at the mill, though practical problems meant that the group moved elsewhere the following year.

Visitors come to the island to watch birds and to look for the otters that

Children constructing a bug hotel.
Photo: M Phillips.

live along the river. One trustee, with the help of other volunteers, built a timber bird-hide at the top of the island that gave a good view of the river, the weir and the canal. It became another target of vandals and was burnt down in March 2020.

Other activities

The building and island have potential to be used for many purposes. RHT is keen to develop the principle of offering a suitable venue for others to provide the training or activity. Having its own hydro systems, it was an obvious venue for the British Hydro Association to use for a training course; the mill and island were used for training teachers in forest school techniques; a writers' group has held several meetings at the mill; a yoga teacher held day-long classes using both the building and the island; and it was a great venue for a children's video-making weekend. During the summers of 2013 and 2014, the mill and island hosted a week-long summer camp for children aged between about 8 and 14 years. The local organiser had experience of summer camps in the USA, and she wanted to replicate the experience here for her own children and others.

One major annual open day has been on the weekend of the national Heritage Open Days (HOD), which is held each September and promoted by English Heritage. The themes chosen for the day have included demonstrating traditional building techniques, the mill as it was when grinding corn and bread-making, and in 2015 a local music festival. Attendance has been as many as the site can cope with, between 150 and 200 people in a day. About 180 came to see the building work in progress during HOD 2012. This followed a 'meet the contractor' weekend on 18/19 August 2012 when Stephen Pickering built a small kiln to make lime mortar that he then used to demonstrate rendering and other techniques to about 200 visitors. RHT has participated in other national events including British Science Week, National Mills Weekend and Climate Week.

Another regular feature has been a Christmas Fair in December. In the early years this was volunteers sharing mulled wine and mince pies around a fire. After completion of the restoration, RHT invited local artisans to sell seasonal items and crafts. For 2015 it was the story behind 'A Christmas Carol' by Charles Dickens, presented in costume and with readings from the book by the Malton Dickens Society.

A fine weekend in February 2016 saw the first of three outdoor theatre

Testing a model waterwheel made by the children.
Photo: M Phillips.

events that year. Hosting outdoor theatre was always an ambition of RHT. Field Trip Arts, a local group, proved it was popular with their show entitled 'Escape to Derwent Island'. Three performances took a total audience of about 150 from the car park onto the island, with scenes acted out at various locations. The play used the natural features of the island and river, combined with tales from the history of the mill to create the story. It was very well received by children and adults alike. Field Trip Arts returned for HOD 2016 to perform 'Flour Power', the dramatised story of some of the millers and their activities.

The Handlebards performing Much Ado about Nothing July 2016.
Photo: M Phillips.

In July of that year, RHT hosted the HandleBards, a four-man Shakespearean bicycle touring group, who put on their take of 'Much Ado about Nothing'. An audience of 90 sat on rugs and deckchairs in front of the east façade of the building, where the actors performed the many parts in this play. It was a balmy summer's evening, ideal for outdoor theatre. The weather was not so favourable in 2017 when the HandleBards returned to perform 'A Midsummer's Night Dream'. Hastily erected cover kept the rain off many, but for others, waterproofs were needed to keep dry. About a quarter of ticket holders decided not to come, for those that did the actors played on undaunted. By now a fixture on their tour, the troupe performed 'Twelfth Night' to a capacity crowd on a fine evening in 2018.

Canoeists are regular visitors to the island throughout the year. There is a chute built in the weir to ride down. Once the wheel was working, local canoe club members strung a series of gates to make a slalom course using the waterwheel outflow. This has become one of the best such sites in Yorkshire. Each July, the mill has hosted a large slalom competition organised by local clubs that attracts about 300 competitors and their supporters from all over the country, people who would not otherwise visit. They are allowed to camp in the adjacent field and enjoy a great social and sporting weekend.

The mill is open on Sundays for guided tours around the building for casual visitors. Numbers coming vary greatly dependent on time of year and weather but can be fifty or more on a warm sunny day. Such visitors are often surprised and pleased to find a guide to talk to them and are consequently very appreciative. For this task RHT has recruited some volunteer guides to help the trustee on duty. Sunday is also a day for maintenance and repair and other volunteers will come to help.

In the years since completing the restoration, about 45 groups have had a guided tour by arrangement, sometimes focussing on their special interest. Trustees have also given off-site talks to a diverse range of groups, some of whom later visited the mill.

A rough estimate of total annual visitors is between 1500 and 2000, though no attempt has been made to count numbers. The island is open all year round for the enjoyment of the peace and quiet of the site, or just for a good place to walk the dog. When the weather is fine, people come to the island to swim in the deep water above the weir. The island is one of the few places along the Derwent where the public is allowed to swim and picnic, by permission of RHT. Sadly, this permission is abused by the littering and petty vandalism of a small minority.

Trustees of the Renewable Heritage Trust and major donors to the project

Howardian Hills Area of Outstanding Natural Beauty
Architectural Heritage Fund
North York Moors National Park Authority
Yorkshire Forward
REACT fund
Ryedale District Council
Buildings at Risk Fund
East Yorkshire Georgian Society
Local Heritage Initiative
Nationwide Building Society
Tim Hall

Volunteers

The restoration of Howsham Mill has been helped by several hundred volunteers, too numerous to name. Some came just for a day, in particular trainee soldiers volunteering as part of their Duke of Edinburgh Bronze award, others have given much time and expertise. Included in the latter category are Bruce Skinner, Elaine Gathercole, Gerry Bradshaw, Dave Bennett, Sue and Simon Hogge, Geraldine Mathieson, Tim and Jane Nicoll, Tony Bartholomew, James Stephenson, Ted Pindar.